AND THE CROWD GOES MILD

AND THE CROWD GOES MILD

CONFESSIONS OF A WORKING MUSICIAN

B. D. LENZ

And the Crowd Goes Mild © 2026 by B.D. Lenz

All rights reserved. No part of this book may be reproduced or transmitted in any form or by any means, electronic or mechanical, without prior written permission from the publisher, except for brief quotations in a review.

Jade Buddha Publishing
Hackettstown, NJ

Library of Congress Control No: 2026928320

ISBN: 979-8-9944379-0-2 (Paperback)
ISBN: 979-8-9944379-2-6 (Hardcover)
ISBN: 979-8-9944379-1-9 (eBook)

~Thank you to my mom for taking me to my first guitar lessons.

~Thank you to Mary Beth, Julia, & Evan for patiently putting up with all this. I'm so grateful for you letting me be me.

~To my musician friends, you are all my heroes.

Contents

Intro i

Chapter 1 - The Entertainer 1

Chapter 2 - Start Me Up 25

Chapter 3 - Sing, Sing, Sing 39

Chapter 4 - Send in the Clowns 47

Chapter 5 - A Day in the Life 69

Chapter 6 - You Can Go Your Own Way 79

Chapter 7 - Leaving On a Jet Plane 95

Chapter 8 - Highway to Hell 111

Chapter 9 - With a Little Help from My Friends 143

Chapter 10 - Taking Care of Business 163

Chapter 11 - The Times They Are A-Changin' 183

Chapter 12 - Don't Stop Believin' 193

Intro

"And the crowd goes mild"—a phrase my bandmates and I have joked countless times over the years after finishing a song, only to be met with the awkward silence of an apathetic audience and the faint clinking of glasses at the bar. It's our way of softening the sting, because if you can't laugh about it, you'll eventually find yourself weeping into your guitar case. This is the *real* music business.

Like most musicians, we didn't imagine it this way. We had the usual rock-and-roll dreams—you know, arenas packed with screaming fans, thunderous applause, maybe a fog machine. Instead, we've all too often found ourselves playing for a disinterested bartender and a guy who thought it was karaoke night. Heck, I once opened for a clown in an empty circus tent. (True story.)

That gap—between what people imagine a musical life to be and what it actually is—is why this story deserves to be told. Most of the public thinks it's all just pyrotechnics, hotel room destruction, and wild parties with ecstatic fans.

I thought so too, once.

Come on, you've seen this story so many times: A misunderstood genius gets discovered in a dive bar, makes a groundbreaking, Grammy-winning album, becomes an overnight sensation, spirals into addiction, discovers betrayal, blows the money on divorces and sports cars—then returns triumphantly with a "raw" comeback album that wins back the public's hearts.

That story gets told plenty. It's sensational, sure—but this book *isn't* that story.

After many years and several thousand gigs, I wanted to write a love letter to the real heroes of the music scene: the everyday musicians working hard on the front lines to make bar mitzvahs and anniversary parties all the more special—to toast the guys churning out covers of "Wonderwall" and "Take Me Home, Country Roads" thousands of times over, so drunken revelers can earnestly slur along. To give a voice to all the bandleaders, sidemen, and road-warriors who show up night after night, providing the soundtrack to everyone else's good times.

Musicians come in all shapes and pay grades. The world of a professional minstrel is a vast continuum, ranging from weekend warriors hacking their way through Rolling Stones covers for $50 and free drinks to well-seasoned, highly educated virtuosos who can read down a score like it's The Matrix. Yet even the most skilled labor is often unseen or anonymous. Take the highly capable professionals in a Broadway pit orchestra—they're some of the best musicians around, yet they remain hidden under a stage. Consider those who play behind famous pop stars; they're often highly accomplished in their own right, yet couldn't be picked out of a lineup. There are even those who compose music for film and TV. You hear their music all the time, but probably never even consider who created it.

Fame doesn't always equal talent, and talent doesn't always bring fame. If that were the case, the pop charts would look very different, and mental health apps would likely go out of business.

Of course, there *are* a lucky few who get that golden ticket to the top. These elite musicians are well-paid and often live a life of private jets and sold-out arenas. I know people like that, and they've earned their success. But for every superstar, there are thousands of us grinding away in the trenches, lugging amps up narrow staircases to play three sets at Joe's Sports Bar.

At the other end of the spectrum, there is the archetypal "broke" musician—you know the kind, where the status of their check engine light doubles as a financial report. That life is all too real, and I know people living it as well. While the reasons for this are probably obvious, I will explore them in more detail in the pages ahead.

What few in the general public recognize, however, are those who live somewhere in between—not rich, not poor. It's the middle class of music, steadily making a living. Yes, that exists. This book shines a spotlight on those mercenaries, whose stories are usually overlooked in favor of grander tales of household names.

It's not about rock gods who caught a lucky break and sell out stadiums. It's about everyday, working-class, blue-collar performers scraping out a living in half-empty bars and at fortieth birthday parties. There are plenty of chronicles devoted to pampered divas who step from their limousines onto stages meticulously prepared by roadies. You'll hear far less about the musicians who shove duct-taped drum kits into hatchbacks a few nights a week, only to painstakingly assemble and disassemble them again and again for a few bucks and an open bar tab.

Me? I live in that middle ground—successful enough to make a living, yet obscure enough that people always ask me, "Why aren't you playing bigger places?" I'm a well-trained guitarist with several thousand gigs under my belt and a few accomplishments I'll brag about later. But I'm not famous. I've never played with anyone you've heard of, and I never landed "the big gig."

For most of my life, I've been a semi-professional musician, working as hard as anyone around me and making a decent living at it—though, truth be told, it was never my only source of income. I also held a day job as a high school math teacher in northern New Jersey for over 25 years. My life consisted of brooding teenagers by day and drunken adults by night—and often, the adults were worse.

I never thought of myself as a teacher with a side hustle. I took music so seriously that, in my mind, I was a musician with a day job. When school colleagues would learn of my other life, they'd hit me with comedy gold like, "Can I join your band? I'll play the tambourine." Hilarious. "Can I be a groupie?" Eye roll. Of course, they all thought they were a hoot—the first ones to think up these side-splitting queries.

When my students inevitably found out, however, their most pressing question was far more serious: "So, are you rich?" Because in their minds, every musician is basically Drake. If only.

(Yes, I'm secretly a billionaire. I teach fractions to teenagers because I find it relaxing.)

That's the funny part. People think that if you've made some albums, you must be rolling in it. And if you've been fortunate enough to do some touring, they imagine it's one long party full of groupies, like a Mötley Crüe video—though entirely understandable, given how musicians are portrayed in music videos and movies. Flashy cars, endless cash, beautiful people—it's all designed to sell the dream.

But in reality?
The cars? Rented.
The cash? Fake.
The people? Constipated.

Ok. That last part was uncalled for. Sorry. I get a little worked up. Deep breath… I'm fine now.

If I sound like I'm bitter, I promise I'm not—just the opposite, in fact. If it sounds like I complain a lot, I prefer to think of it as "artistic expression." Honesty is refreshing, so I've been told.

I want this exploration to be real, with no pretense or artifice. And, while some of the observations I'll share might seem like I'm poking fun at those crazy enough to pursue this life, they're actually told with genuine affection. I admire the indomitable souls willing to endure its absurdities to follow their passion. Musicians are a quirky bunch, and I love that about them, but you almost have to be a bit bonkers to chase this muse. It's devotion, it's hardship, it's chaos, and it's joy. And while many of us have secretly googled "how to fake your death and re-emerge as an accountant," most wouldn't trade this life for anything.

In the pages ahead, I'll pull back the curtain on a life in music—the good, the bad, and the gloriously uncomfortable. Maybe you'll leave with a deeper appreciation for the unsung musical warriors. Perhaps it'll even give you pause before shouting, "Freebird" or "More cowbell" at some underpaid combo doing their best to entertain a crowd. Yes, it can be exciting, fun, and rewarding to play music, but it can also make you grit your teeth every time someone says, "You're so lucky—you get to *do what you love!*"

1

The Entertainer

Over the years, I've played thousands of gigs in more bands than most people have had bad relationships. Each one of them has taught me something about the job, the music, and entertaining people. Our occupation is extremely interconnected with our customers—the audience—and how my night goes depends a lot on the people for whom we're playing. If they're loving it, I'm loving it. If they're not? Well, that's when things get... character building. I can't say there have been many occasions where the audience has *hated* it. But as some of my later stories will illustrate, it's happened.

Honestly, the most common reaction, by far, is indifference—like we're wallpaper with instruments. I've become quite accustomed to being ignored, and while it's discouraging, I've developed a thick skin and no longer take it personally. It doesn't mean I'm not good at what I do, or even that an audience doesn't like the music. But when a crowd *is* into it, I'll pour my heart out. The old saying, "an audience gets the performance they deserve," is spot on.

The size of the audience doesn't make much of a difference to me anymore, either. I'll take a small but enthusiastic crowd over a large, apathetic one any day. For me, it's all about connection. Sure, I want every venue to be successful, but I've played for two people, and I've played for thousands, and I'm going to give my best regardless of how many people are there to see it. People have endless ways to spend their time these days, and I feel a real responsibility to make sure it's worth their while—especially if they've gone out of their way to be there.

In theory, our relationship with a crowd *should* be a simple one: We perform, they listen or dance, and, if they like it, they show their appreciation with claps, cheers, and "woos"—a straightforward transactional occurrence. In practice, though, it's not always that clear-cut. Venues, expectations, alcohol, and misunderstanding can complicate things quickly.

Throughout my career, I've encountered a recurring cast of characters who—intentionally or not—make live music harder than it needs to be. We all know there are difficult people with whom every profession must deal.

Allow me to enlighten you on the nuisances we *musicians* face by introducing a brief field guide to the People Ruining In-Concert Koolness—P.R.I.C.K.s, if you will—along with a few tips on how to avoid joining their ranks.

Exhibit A: Sir Hush-a-Lot

The most common example of bad audience behavior comes in the form of the complainer; there's always one, and it's usually about volume. It happens all the time and can range anywhere from someone coming up and asking politely, "Excuse me. Do you mind turning it down a smidge?" to some crazed psycho screaming, "I CAN'T HEAR MYSELF THINK!" (Well, sir, that's probably a good thing).

Don't get me wrong—we *do* get too loud, and it's ok for people to let us know. But it's happened in situations where we're barely touching our instruments. It's like, *Why did you even hire a band then? Are we just cool decorations?* We're so afraid our "racket" will make Uncle Chester choke on his lobster bisque that we might as well turn the amps off.

And when it's *finally* time to take our break, they'll put on house music that's even louder than we were. Figure that one out!

How *not* to be that person: Before complaining, consider whether your seat or expectations might be part of the issue. And if you're hoping for the ambiance of a hospital waiting room, live music may not be the right fit.

Exhibit B: The Jukebox Jockey

Another variety of complainer is the person unhappy with the musical selections, and I have a lot to say on this topic. Song requests are an occupational hazard. Most are harmless—someone wants to hear their wedding song or a tune that reminds them of their college days. I get that. But some people assume that just because you're a professional band, you know every song in existence, regardless of genre, and that you should only be playing their favorites. In this case, they'll either make obscure requests or just plain bad ones.

Like, *No, I've never heard the Smiths track from their B-side Japanese release. Even if I had, I'm pretty sure this wedding isn't the appropriate place to play it.*

Or, *Yes, I do know the "Electric Slide," but I still have a small shred of dignity left. Although I've had to sacrifice most of it for this gig, I'm still holding on to that last tiny bit and not play that turd of a song.*

There's always some guy who insists he knows what song you *should* play next. He'll approach between songs, brimming with confidence, and say something like "You should do 'Sweet Home Alabama'—people love that one," as if it's a revelation. I nod, thank him for the suggestion, then continue doing my job, while thinking, *Yes, sir, your musical genius is duly noted, as if I couldn't already tell by those blazing "air guitar" solos you do.*

Also, just because I've heard a song doesn't mean the band can instantly come together and play it. Don't get me wrong—we'll try, and we have—but don't expect it. Sometimes people are incredulous, or even downright angry, that we don't know a particular song. Picture this in an "up talk" manner of speaking: "What do you mean you don't know 'Simple' by Katy Perry? You've never heard that song?" There are millions of songs in existence, and oddly, I don't know every one of them. If I hadn't needed to learn your song by this point in my career, it must not be *that* famous (or good).

It's common for someone to request a song that we're simply ill-equipped to play. For example, we'll be playing as a jazz trio, and someone will want to hear Bruce Springsteen when we don't even have a singer. Now, we've gotten pretty good at pulling off cover songs as an instrumental band, but they're likely not going to sound the way the audience wants to hear it. In fact, it would probably be inappropriate at the baby's christening we're playing. On the other hand, if your request comes with a $20 bill attached, "Born to Run" will suddenly become "Born to Try."

For weddings, I usually tell the couple we'll learn two songs not in our repertoire. In most cases, they make good choices with romantic or classic songs. However, sometimes the selections are baffling, particularly for a couple sharing their nuptials. I always have to remind them that their grandparents will probably be there, so "Baby Got Back" might not be the best choice.

One of the funniest instances occurred at a wedding we were hired for where the notably "emo" couple requested a song by the English rock band The Cure. They're not on my list of favorite bands, but that doesn't matter; it wasn't about me.

I should mention that my singer, Justin, is a Black dude who can sing the hell out of Stevie Wonder. He's very soulful but can also belt out any rock tune when asked. This was the first time I'd ever seen him stumped. The poor guy tried, too. Listening to him attempt to sound like a white, British new waver was hilarious. Personally, I think he sounded like Kermit the Frog.

While on the topic of requests, my jazz group is often hired to play at events by people who know very little about music, let alone jazz. Their requests can be very odd. Once, a woman hired my band for an event and asked if I could bring someone who played the "golden clarinet like Kenny G." Bless her—Kenny G plays a soprano saxophone, but close enough. I mean, it's straight like a clarinet, but it's still a saxophone. I understand that not everyone knows the difference, but a question like that is the kind of red flag that lets you know it's likely the first in a long series of puzzling demands.

Every so often, someone asks for a song that instantly sets off my internal eye-roll. This confession never wins me any friends: I'm not exactly a fan of the Grateful Dead. I know, blasphemy! They just never did it for me. However, at certain gigs, some guy will come up and ask, "Dude, know any Dead?" I was a Boy Scout, and their motto is "be prepared," so I happen to know one simple song that I always keep in my back pocket for *just* such an occasion. It's called "Franklin's Tower," and I've had to play it too many times now. I also know one Elvis song, just in case ("I Can't Help Falling In Love With You"). On several occasions, we've played at parties that have been interrupted by local police enforcing noise ordinances. These instances always compel us to break into the theme song to the TV show *Cops*. "Bad boys, bad boys. Whatcha gonna do? Whatcha gonna do when they come for you?" Thankfully, everyone has found it amusing (so far), including the police themselves.

As a working musician, you begin to mark the calendar by the songs you're expected to know. Every holiday comes with its own signature soundtrack. Any gig in December, for instance, requires having a few Christmas classics on hand. Want to hear "Frosty the Snowman" or "Silver Bells"? Sure, I know those. New Year's Eve? "Auld Lang Syne." Valentine's Day? "My Funny Valentine." St. Patrick's Day? "Danny Boy." Mardi Gras? "When the Saints Go Marching In." Halloween? "Thriller." Independence Day? "America the Beautiful." Yup, I've got you covered. But there's one song that's essential in any setting, any season. You're not a true musician unless you have "Happy Birthday" locked and loaded, ready to fire off at a moment's notice. Beware—this one often gets called for with little to no warning. Sometimes all you see is a glowing cake emerging from the kitchen, and suddenly it's "go time" for that timeless chestnut. Take it from this Boy Scout: be prepared.

How *not* to be that person: Remember that a live band isn't Spotify Premium, and part of the experience is hearing what *they've* chosen to play. As for song requests like "Don't Stop Believin'," rest assured—we know. People love that one. We are aware.

Exhibit C: The Dancing Queen

Another common offender is the woman who patronizingly asks, "Can you guys play something I can dance to?" Forget that it's a formal dinner and we've been hired to provide quiet background jazz. Or that we're just a guitar and saxophone duo ill-equipped to provide a proper dance beat; *she* wants to "dance like nobody's watching," as if two musicians could drown out the disappointment of her last three marriages. So we have to ignore everyone else's wishes, including those of the insurance company that hired us.

How *not* to be that person: Sometimes the best way to enjoy the music is simply to sit back and listen. Enjoy a quiet dinner for once. A live performance can be a great opportunity to relax and enjoy some conversation while the music unfolds. Remember, we're two musicians creating something in real time—not a drum machine, a horn section, and a time machine to 1970s Studio 54.

Exhibit D: The Steven Spielberg Wannabe

My next target is people taking videos with their cellphones. First of all, some folks will take videos of anything these days. That, in and of itself, is generally not a problem. It *becomes* a problem, however, when they happen to catch what we think is a bad performance and "generously" share that bad performance on YouTube. It sucks, but there's nothing you can do about it; it's just the world we live in nowadays. I'll take some of the blame for not playing as well as I had hoped.

However, what *truly* irritates me is when people walk up to us, push their phones in our faces, and hold them there for an extended period of time. It's a complete distraction and obstructs some of the audience's view. If that weren't bad enough, people sometimes shine their cameras' light on us, particularly in a dark venue.

I'm trying to concentrate and be inside the music so I can give my best performance, but that's disrupted entirely when a tractor beam is shot right in my eyes, as if I'm about to be lifted into a UFO mothership. I'm sorry, but as much as you're trying to be artsy, your video probably won't get more than 10 likes on Instagram.

How *not* to be that person: Don't film a band like you're documenting Bigfoot. A little breathing room helps everyone enjoy the moment—performers included.

Exhibit E: Ugh…This Guy

The culprits listed above are egregious, but there's one audience member who rises above all others and is easily the most maddening: the individual who needs to be addressed. Corporal punishment should be administered against him. The most irritating spectator by far is the drunk guy at the back of the bar who thinks he's a comedic trailblazer by shouting "Freebird" or "More cowbell," ad nauseam. It happens more than you might think. That might've been funny for about a week in 2000, but its shelf life expired long ago, and it's just not that amusing anymore. For reasons unknown, he's convinced his 'clever' line is a masterstroke that will finally win him some female admirers.

How *not* to be that person: If you really feel the need to yell from the back of the bar, make it something we would all appreciate, like, "Hey bartender, this round of drinks is on me."

Exhibit F: Haters be Hatin'

Whether we're there to entertain or lay low in the background, performing for people can earn praise and applause. It can just as easily make you a target for those who think it's ok to say awful things. On one occasion, we were playing some pleasant jazz in a high-end department store when a guy came over and said, "Good job playing for yourself. Why don't you play something for the people here?"

First of all, what does that even mean? I think he was suggesting that we were ignoring what people in the store might want to hear. Yes, we were playing music we liked, but we're pretty good at reading the room; we were only hired to play quiet shopping music, and most people didn't care anyway. Although, you genuinely have to feel sorry for a guy who finds it necessary to berate musicians between sock purchases.

Truthfully, the haters don't bother me much anymore. One thing I've learned over the years is that you can't please everyone all the time. There's always *someone* who's going to be unhappy about something you're playing, and they'll be sure to let you know about it. I'm certain that people who work in the service industry deal with this much more often than I ever will. At this point, I don't let one unhappy person spoil my night, especially when there's a room full of content listeners.

How *not* to be that person: You don't need to wander over in the middle of a performance and give your Yelp review. Thoughtful comments afterward are always appreciated, but I wouldn't show up at your job and say, "Good job filing those taxes for yourself—why not file them for the people?"

Exhibit G: Mr. Chatterbox

There are ways to be inconsiderate besides making unpleasant comments or bad requests. Sometimes people will walk up in the middle of a song and try to start a conversation with me. When I'm playing, my hands are occupied, and my head is in the music. Could they at least wait until I'm finished with the song? But even then, they often want to have an in-depth discussion with me about whether I know their cousin who plays drums in a local metal band while my bandmates impatiently wait for me to stop talking and the audience has to endure awkward silence with no music. That's not the best time to engage in such discourse.

Please don't misunderstand—I *do* enjoy talking with people, at appropriate times, like during a set break or after the gig. It's part of the job to connect with the crowd, and I like catching up with people I haven't seen in a while. As much of a shy and introverted person as I am, I've become amazingly comfortable performing and speaking in front of large audiences. Not much fazes me anymore. I'm actually *more* anxious when talking to people individually, as I always feel the pressure to be a good host.

But I admit that sometimes, when I simply want to decompress and clear my head, it's frustrating when some guy is dying to talk to me about the '69 Stratocaster he owns or the band he was in 20 years ago. If I'm being perfectly honest, these conversations can be tiresome. I'm generally not into discussing musical gear or hearing about someone's '90s progressive rock band, "Proton." But I remind myself that while I've had these conversations hundreds of times before, this person hasn't. If I've excited them about music or playing guitar, that's what I wanted to do, so I'm happy to listen.

When you've moved someone in a meaningful way, they'll sometimes come up and pour their hearts out. I've met folks who have been very emotional, wanting to tell me how a particular piece of music meant so much to them or even divulge a hardship they're going through. I've come to realize that touching them so profoundly allows them to feel like they can open up and talk about things that are very personal to them.

Even if I'm tired and can't wait to pack up and go home, I'll stay and listen. Clearly, they have something they want to share, and I'm honored that they feel comfortable sharing it with me.

How *not* to be that person: It's best to wait until a set break to chat. And, if you're going to give me a TED Talk, at least bring a beer for both of us.

Exhibit H: Captain Cuckoo

Music has a way of bringing out the crazy in people. On one occasion, we were playing outside at a farmer's market in downtown Newark, New Jersey, which is a pretty rough city. A diverse cross-section of humanity was gathered at the market, from businessmen on lunch breaks to homeless people enjoying a sunny day.

We were playing next to some vegetable stands when, out of nowhere, a grubby-looking, superhero wannabe came running up wearing only a pair of jeans and a cape. No shirt, no shoes. One by one, he got right up in our faces and stared intensely into each of our eyes. It was the most uncomfortable minute I'd ever experienced. I think I left my body and saw Buddha. Then, just like that, he took off and disappeared back into the crowd.

Just another day at the office.

How *not* to be that person: If you genuinely need guidance on this one, it might be time for a little self-reflection.

Exhibit I: We See You

Perhaps you think "seeing" is a one-way street, with the audience watching us, the band. Well, I'm here to tell you it works both ways. We watch them too. It's great to witness enthusiastic people who make us feel good about what we're doing. But we also can't help but notice weird people doing weird things, and we'll almost certainly laugh about those people amongst ourselves on the next set break.

It is also interesting to observe how people react when they hear music. If it feels good, most people will unconsciously move some part of their body, whether it's tapping a toe, drumming their fingers, nodding their heads, or even shaking their booty. That's often a subtle tip that we're doing something right. I know when I hear something I like, I start drumming with my hands or fingers. Everyone's reaction is different.

I especially enjoy watching people during an audience-participation segment, noting who can clap in time and who struggles to keep a simple beat. Some people naturally have more rhythm or "soul," while others have to try especially hard. And let's be honest—some people can really dance, and some... have "interesting techniques." I'm sorry, but if you dance like your hips *do* lie, we're probably going to laugh about that later, too.

Full disclosure: I can't dance either, but at least I have the self-awareness not to get down in the center of the dance floor. Or maybe I'm just too sober.

How *not* to be that person: Nahh. Just ignore my smug sarcasm. You do *you*!

Exhibit J: Look, Don't Touch

Next are the "musicians" who assume we're all "bros" and it's totally ok to walk up and start playing our instruments during our break. They'll just pick up the drumsticks and start playing the drum kit without permission. It's a bit presumptuous to say the least, but it's even worse when *non*-musicians do this.

There have been more than a few times when a young kid has walked up to my bass player's 18th-century German upright bass and started playing on it like a jungle gym while their parent stands there, fawning over their adorable angel. It's too expensive an instrument to be assaulted like that, yet they assume that everyone else also thinks it's the cutest thing.

How *not* to be that person: Instruments on stage shouldn't be treated like a petting zoo, and the best time to touch a band's gear is when they say, 'Hey, want to touch our gear?'"

Exhibit K: Bro, Let's Jam!

We're regularly approached by people who claim to be musicians and want to jam with us by requesting to "sit in" with the band. Accepting that proposition is like rolling the dice. We've had some great guests and some dreadfully bad ones. I'm always a bit reluctant to let folks join us for that very reason.

I was once on a gig in New Jersey, and Snooki, a famed cast member of MTV's *Jersey Shore*, was there with her then-boyfriend. Her bodyguard approached us and asked if she could play the drums with us. Of course, we agreed, but I had no idea what to expect. Well, apparently, she had never sat behind a drum kit before, and all hope of playing music was over for the evening.
On another occasion, we were serenading a cocktail party at an affluent country club in northern New Jersey. The environment was quite stuffy, and we were playing quiet background jazz so members could close their real estate deals. An extremely drunk

club member walked up and stammered, "Hey...hey...*hey*. Could I play drums with you guys for one s-s-s-song?" With my usual skepticism, I asked, "Do you know how to play the drums?" He replied, "Yes, and I'm really g-g-g-good." I wasn't convinced, but he *was* a member of the club, and I was trying to make a good impression to get more work there. I looked over at my drummer, who graciously gave up his drumsticks and moved aside while this gentleman stumbled behind the kit. I asked the man, "What would you like to play?" and he responded with complete confidence, "I can p-p-play anything." Anything? Wow! Maybe he was that good, but the intoxicated glimmer in his eyes made me second-guess my decision.

Staying appropriate to the evening, I said, "How about the standard 'All of Me'? We'll swing it, but we'll need to keep it really quiet." Again, he was full of assurances. "That's not a p-p-problem." With short-lived mental comfort, I snapped my fingers and counted off the song: "Uh-one, uh-two, uh-one, two, three..." But just as the word "four" exited my mouth, he began bashing on the drum kit, and I mean *bashing*—every drum and cymbal available to him. There was nothing musical about it, nothing skillful, just pounding like a caveman. Instantly, every person in the room stopped what they were doing and glared at us, horrified and disgusted by the racket emanating from our corner of the room.

This "drumming" continued for about a minute, which felt like an eternity, as I begged him to please stop playing. Eventually, he relented. As you might imagine, I never played there again.

How *not* to be that person: Remember that you weren't called to play this gig for a reason. The world will still be alright if you refrain from sharing your musical genius at every opportunity.

Exhibit L: You're Cut Off

I'm sure it comes as no surprise that drunk audience members are prone to bad behavior. I've seen plenty of fights as well as people who've been bounced out of clubs. I even watched a dude get dragged out of a bar before being tased on the pavement by security. Still, I've rarely felt unsafe. I'm a peaceful person and haven't been in a fight since I was 12.

However, we were once playing at a jazz club in Belgium when a group of drunk British guys came in. One of them was completely hammered, leaned against a wall *right* next to me, and stared at me while I was performing. He was invading my personal space and slurring incoherent nonsense. Because of the way he looked at me combined with his proximity, I genuinely felt threatened. I had to stop playing in the middle of a song, get nose-to-nose with him, and say, "Get the fuck out of my face," at which point his friends dragged him out of there. I had never done that before, and it was entirely out of character for me, but he definitely brought out the "Jersey" in me. Tony Soprano would be proud.

How *not* to be that person: Don't believe that alcohol always makes you funnier or more charming. Sometimes it turns you into the reason that security practices takedown drills.

Exhibit M: Hello? Is Anyone Out There?

It's always baffling when patrons offer no reaction whatsoever and are little more than a blank slate. A lot of what I do and the songs I choose are based, at least in part, on the response we're getting from our audience, whether consciously or unconsciously. They usually make it abundantly clear how they feel about the music; their body language says it all. I believe I'm adept at reading a crowd, and, for certain gigs, I use this skill as a gauge to assess where the night might go in terms of song selection and vibe. That's why I prefer not to make a setlist in advance; I like to pick songs as we go so we can match the audience's energy.

Sometimes, however, you can't get anything out of them no matter what you do; they just seem completely indifferent. They're not looking at us, they're not singing along, their bodies aren't moving, nothing. There have even been instances of people with earbuds in, listening to something else entirely, which is a little insulting. But it's fine; I've been doing this long enough that I don't need everyone's approval.

I will admit that my bands basically run two entirely different setlists. One is for the folks who are actually paying attention—leaning in, listening, genuinely engaged. The other is for people who clearly just wanted pleasant background noise for their conversations about mortgages, kids, and whatever Rachel did *this* time.

If the crowd's locked in and we want to entertain them, we break out what we lovingly call our "shit-they-know" set. You know—songs that are a little louder, a little brighter, and statistically guaranteed to make at least three people say, "Ohhh, I love this one!"

If they're not paying attention, we shift to our "shit-they-don't-know" set. That's when we basically say, "Cool, we'll just play for ourselves then." Maybe it's a jazz standard I've been shedding; maybe it's some obscure pop tune we dust off once every presidential administration. Hey, we'll simply do what we do and entertain ourselves, so at least someone is having fun.

But I can't tell you how many times I've played to a crowd that seems completely aloof, yet will come up afterward and say something like "Your performance blew me away. I loved it." Really? I would never have guessed.

That's why I no longer let an audience's seeming indifference bother me. While it's always nice to get positive feedback in the moment, some folks are simply more reserved and less demonstrative in their appreciation. So I've learned not to assume anything. Indifference is some people's standing ovation.

Ok, Deep breath. After unloading all of that, it needs to be said: most audiences are great. Sure, some are strange, some are quiet, some are awkward—but many are generous, thoughtful, and deeply appreciative in ways that don't always announce themselves loudly. Each crowd has its own mood and personality, and it's our job to meet it with our own.

When the Crowd Steals the Show

Occasionally, the crowd even becomes the most memorable part of the gig. Now, let me tell you about a few I'll never forget.

Once, I was accompanying a children's singer at an elementary school. I've only done one of these gigs, but it revealed to me a fundamental difference between boys and girls. As you'd expect, the songs were silly and fun, and encouraged lots of audience participation. As we began our set, the kids sat nicely on their mats and shyly participated, at first. Then, they grew more confident as they became more comfortable.

As the show went on and the kids grew even more excited, they began standing up to dance, jump around, and get downright rowdy. By the end, all the girls were holding hands and moving around in a nice circle like "Ring Around the Rosie," while the boys were running around wildly, ramming into each other like they were getting an introduction to moshing. For me, the contrast was a sociological case study on gender.

An audience can always surprise you. I briefly played with an Israeli singer/pianist in New York City. He could be difficult, but I liked his songs and the other members of his band. He told us about a particular gig he'd booked at a hot new club in SoHo, excited to have landed a coveted Thursday night slot. Although the performance was at night, we had to set up and soundcheck earlier in the day.

I arrived at what looked like a pretty standard nightclub, albeit empty and lifeless during the

And the Crowd Goes Mild

daytime. TVs lined the perimeter, and we set up in a loft overlooking the space. After soundcheck, we went our separate ways until gig time.

When I came back hours later, the place was absolutely jam-packed. It was indeed a popular place, but the guy-to-girl ratio was suspiciously lopsided. I didn't see the bandleader until it was show time, and just as the band launched into the first song, he came strolling out in a very flamboyant outfit highlighted by a studded pink cowboy hat. Things were beginning to make sense. Just as I started to process the situation, all the TVs in the club flickered on, showing *male adult programming*. (Was that even legal?)

Yup, suspicions confirmed. Needless to say, there was a long line to get into the men's bathroom that night.

On another occasion, I was playing a solo guitar gig in front of a nice hotel in Bethlehem, Pennsylvania, just as live music was starting to make a comeback after the COVID pandemic. Everyone still had to sit outside at that time, and I was playing for customers dining at the restaurant. I noticed that the people at the table next to me were enjoying my performance and generously expressed their appreciation. As I looked more closely, I noticed that they were the cast of "American Pickers," a reality TV show on the History Channel, and they were staying at the hotel. One of the prominent cast members asked me to play some songs that I didn't know. He kept shouting them out until, finally, he landed on one that I *did* know. Relieved, I played it for him, and he tipped me $50! What a nice group of people they were.

I've played for plenty of well-known actors, athletes, and other celebrities, and while famous people don't make me nervous, notable *musicians* often do.

Quite recently, I was performing with a jazz trio at the Jersey Shore when a guy walked up to us between songs and told us how much he loved what we were doing. He had a $100 bill in his hand and asked if we had a tip jar. I thought he looked familiar and asked if he was a musician, too. He ignored my question and continued to tell my drummer how much he loved the way he played. I pressed him, "Aren't you a musician?" He seemed embarrassed by the question but sheepishly answered, "Yeah, I sing in a band called Train." I knew it! Pat Monahan is a super cool guy, but I'm glad I didn't notice him before he approached us or I might have fangirled a little too much.

Speaking of musicians, I can always tell when there's another guitar player in the audience. Perhaps it's the folded arms, scrutinizing scowl, and continuous gaze at my left hand that gives it away. My suspicions are always confirmed afterward when they come to look at my guitar pedals and ask questions like "Which op-amp chip is in your Tube Screamer? Is it the TS7 or the TS9 model? Is it Keeley-modded?" If you have no idea what I just said, don't worry; I don't either, and I'm not particularly interested in chatting about it.

Another time, my jazz group performed at Musikfest, a festival in eastern Pennsylvania, where we played the classic Curtis Mayfield ballad "People Get Ready." In the middle of my guitar solo, I heard the drums drop out briefly, but didn't think much of it.

And the Crowd Goes Mild

When I finished and was passing it off to my sax player, I looked behind me to find the legendary drummer Bernard Purdie (who played with Aretha Franklin, Steely Dan, etc.) sitting behind the kit. He's unmistakable. Every aspiring drummer is familiar with the "Purdie Shuffle," and there he was. I was confused but thrilled. It turned out that he was playing in the band after us and jumped in when he heard this soul classic. I was glad he did, but was also relieved that I hadn't known in advance or I'd have been extremely nervous.

As a postscript, a few months later, I ran into him at a music convention, and I said, "Hey Bernard, good to see you again. You sat in with my band a few months ago at Musikfest." His excited response: "I don't remember that." Oh well, I guess that moment won't make it into *his* book.

Truth be told, for every P.R.I.C.K. in the crowd, there's someone who's genuine and sincere who restores your faith in humanity. On many occasions, I've walked into a venue full of folded arms and skeptical looks, only to leave with those same people cheering and singing my praises. It can be a battle sometimes, but when you win, it's all the more validating.

Despite all my grumbling, most audiences genuinely appreciate what we do and are generous with their gratitude, often stopping by afterward to say kind things. Just recently, a woman approached me after a solo guitar gig and said, "Thank you for bringing everyone here some happiness." I was genuinely touched by her thoughtful words; they were nice to hear. One kind comment like that can erase ten nasty ones.

Be *that* person.

2

Start Me Up

I grew up in the mostly white, rural suburbs of northern New Jersey, where "diverse music" meant tuning in to both AM and FM radio. My parents listened to some artists they liked, but I didn't encounter much variety. Looking back, my exposure to music was like white bread—plain, functional, and ultimately just a vehicle for something tastier.

Even so, I was always drawn to music. As a kid, I loved listening closely, trying to understand how songs worked. I was mainly into pop songs on the radio until I was twelve, when my brother turned me on to the Canadian progressive rock trio Rush (cue angelic choir). Along with U2, Led Zeppelin, Pink Floyd, and Jimi Hendrix, I mostly listened to the Mount Rushmore of "classic rock." But Rush became my religion. They were intelligent, weird, sophisticated, and original. Also, I'll admit it: I'm a nerd. But they made me want to pick up an instrument.

Excalibur in a Cardboard Case

I started on the alto saxophone in the school band. That was...okay. I enjoyed it enough, but I never practiced. When I did, my parents would wince at the awful honks and squeaks coming out of it.

A few years later, when I was in the eighth grade, our middle school music teacher purchased an electric bass guitar and asked if anyone wanted to play it. I was eager to try something cooler than the sax, so I raised my hand. I was given the Mel Bay Electric Bass Method, Volume 1, and was told to go figure it out. The music was simple. But I loved being at the back of the stage, all by myself, on my own musical island of sorts. I wasn't just another saxophone player; I was *the* bass player. Nobody else knew how to play it, and I felt special having those low-end frequencies all to myself.

After school, however, reality hit. I nearly broke my back trying to lug the damn thing home. In its case, it was enormous, about as tall as I was. I remember the struggle of carrying it just a few feet, and the annoyance of my schoolmates when I would smash their shins lugging it to the back of the school bus. But hey, I knew I'd have to step on a few people along the path to rock stardom.

I played bass for that year only, and then returned to the sax when I entered high school the following year. But my world changed forever when, just a few months later, my uncle gave me his old electric guitar. It was '70s brown, and the case was made of flimsy cardboard, but it might as well have been Excalibur. It was like giving an addict his first high, and I'd remain a junkie (so to speak) for the rest of my life. Everything else in my life fell by the wayside.

Sports? Gone.
Friends? Optional.
Sleep? Overrated.

It was always in my hands, and I often fell asleep with it mid-strum. I couldn't learn enough about it, so my mom paid for lessons at a local music store, and I started by learning some basic rock songs. I still remember being introduced to the *power chord* and learning "Rock You Like a Hurricane" by the Scorpions. I soon bought a distortion pedal and was officially ready to *rawk*!

I still played the saxophone in the school band, but once I became a guitarist, that poor thing never came home with me again. We didn't exactly break up—we just decided it was better to stay friends.

Toward the end of high school, I faced a crossroads. I was torn between music school and flight school. I applied for an ROTC scholarship and decided to let fate choose. Had I received it, I'd be flying jets instead of playing guitar. (Spoiler alert: you'll learn nothing about airplanes in this book.)

Master Class in Tinsel Town

So, music school it would be. Immediately after high school, I moved to the other side of the country to attend Musicians Institute in Hollywood, California. That campus is not just "in Hollywood," it's just off Hollywood Boulevard itself, the famous street with all the stars on it, the flame to which all the craziest moths are drawn. Coming from rural Northern New Jersey, this place was like another planet, and I had to learn street smarts quite quickly. Hollywood in the late '80s wasn't the Disney-esque family tourist spot it is today. It was a seedy place, full of seedy people, and it forced me to grow up quickly.

At M.I., I quickly learned that being the best guitarist in high school doesn't mean squat. I thought I was a hotshot because I could play Jimi Hendrix's "Purple Haze" better than anyone I knew, but I was in for a rude awakening. This was 1989, at the tail end of the L.A. "hair metal" scene, with the likes of Ratt, Mötley Crüe, and Ozzy Osbourne, so "shredding" was all the rage.

I liked some of that music a lot; I grew up on it. It was a rare time in history when guitar virtuosity was on the pop charts. But that scene wasn't for me, and I felt somewhat out of place as one of the few people at school with short hair—innocent of all Aqua-net related ozone depletion.

I really didn't know *what* I wanted to do; I just knew I wanted to learn everything I could about the guitar and how to make a living playing it. I was quite green when school started. Despite my musical knowledge, I had minimal experience playing in bands and limited exposure to other musical styles. I learned so

And the Crowd Goes Mild

much there that it was almost overwhelming. Every day, I watched some of the most outstanding musicians perform concerts and teach master classes, giving me a clear picture of what it takes to be a pro. Music school was a great experience, but it was also a whirlwind of knowledge, and I struggled to take it all in.

During this time, I got to perform with a very famous band... well, sort of. As a broke student, I took every opportunity to make a few bucks—including being an extra in TV and films. C'mon, it's Hollywood! If you're not familiar, extras are those people awkwardly milling around in the background, pretending they belong. It was fun, and I even landed a few commercials and a tiny spot in the legendary *Pretty Woman*—which, of course, ended up on the cutting room floor.

Then came my "big break": a commercial with a "famous band." I showed up, buzzing with excitement... only to discover it was a Coca-Cola ad with New Kids on the Block, the absolute hottest thing in music at the time. I was just another anonymous face in a fake concert crowd—until lunchtime, when the director handpicked five of us to stand in as body doubles. For a few glorious takes, I was "hanging tough" with the New Kids... but fame is fleeting. After my brief taste of stardom, it was back to school, back to the practice room.

No, teen-pop wasn't for me. It was actually jazz that crept into my life. At first, I didn't get it. There were too many weird notes and not nearly enough distortion. But as I heard more of it around school, my curiosity grew. I didn't come to it the way many do, through pioneers like Miles Davis, John Coltrane, or Thelonious Monk—that appreciation came later. Instead, I was lured in by jazz-rock guitarists, who served as a "gateway drug." Listening to the likes of virtuoso guitarist Scott Henderson jamming in a little practice room will show you the light.

I even saw a concert at school by the great "jazz fusion" guitarist Mike Stern (who had famously played with Miles Davis), but I remember walking away not understanding what I'd just heard. I wasn't ready for that yet. *Later*, he became one of my biggest heroes and, in a full-circle moment, played on one of my albums. But I'm getting ahead of myself.

Cultivating the Garden State

After a year of absorbing everything Hollywood could throw at me, I needed a place to catch my breath—a way to practice and postpone adulthood without the pressure of getting a "real job." I returned to New Jersey and enrolled at The College of New Jersey, majoring in math education, not out of passion, but efficiency. Math came easily, which left plenty of time to practice. I went to class in the mornings and then vanished into my dorm room, holed up with chords, scales, songs, and my first attempts at writing music. My floormates even nicknamed me "floor ghost" because nobody ever saw me. Disciplined or antisocial? Potato, potahto.

People often ask why I didn't become a *music* teacher. I've been asked that a lot. The answer is, I never wanted to *teach* music; I just wanted to play it. Teaching kids how to play "Hot Crossed Buns" wasn't my jam, and I didn't want to learn the flute or tuba; I just wanted to learn everything I could about guitar. No disrespect to music teachers. They are saints, and their work is a blessing, but that path wasn't for me.

I wanted to join a band, so I started looking for musicians my age to jam with. I was open to anything promising, but I was especially eager to play jazz, given how much the genre had excited me at music school. In the era of Nirvana and Pearl Jam, finding like-minded players wasn't easy, but I connected with some guys from nearby music schools and began writing and recording a few original tunes with them. The compositions were immature, and the recordings crude, but it was a start.

Incidentally, one of the musicians I met and began playing with at that time was drummer Brendan Buckley. Brendan later moved to L.A. to play with the likes of Shakira, Morrissey, and Perry Farrell. Not too shabby.

Welcome to Music Inc.

After graduating from TCNJ with a B.A. in mathematics education, a minor in music, and a PhD in practicing guitar, I was now ready to face the world, but had no idea how to start a music career. You don't just apply for gigs by sending out a resume to "Music Incorporated." Although I imagine the interview process would have gone something like this:

Interviewer: "Welcome to Music Inc. Why do you want to work here?"
Candidate: "I'm seeking emotional instability, inconsistent income, and long hours in poorly lit spaces."
Interviewer: "What are you looking for in terms of compensation?"
Candidate: "Will you validate my parking?"
Interviewer: "Where do you see yourself in five years?"
Candidate: "Explaining to my family that this is still my job."
Interviewer: "Lastly, do you have a drug or alcohol problem?"
Candidate: "Not yet, but I understand that can be arranged."
Interviewer: "Yes, it can be. Welcome aboard."

If only. Soooo…what *do* you do? In 1995, there was no real internet to speak of, so I went to the local New Jersey music rag called "The Aquarian"—the Craigslist of its day—to scour the "musicians wanted" ads in the back. These were hilariously stupid.

> **Wanted: Musicians to Shred, Growl, and Melt Faces!**
> Battle Axe seeks a heavy-metal maniac influenced by Metallica, Iron Maiden, and that Viking-looking dude from the local bar. Must tolerate loud rehearsals, tight leather pants, fog machines, and—ideally—own a cape. All instruments considered. Heck, even a kazoo, if you can make it sound evil.

I answered ads for all kinds of bands and found most of their members to be incredibly flaky or highly dysfunctional in some notable way. But I was determined, so I went to lots of auditions. Heck, I even played with an Elvis impersonator for a brief time—playing guitar solos while ducking karate moves took some getting used to. But after two gigs, Elvis left the building and moved to Texas, so I went back to the ads, and one of them finally paid off.

Key of C...as in Confusion

I landed my first professional gig with a four-piece outfit called Super Fresh. Despite its tantalizing name, there was nothing "super" or "fresh" about this group. This was in the mid-'90s, and we played corny versions of mostly '70s music.

The band was led by a middle-aged, curly-haired keyboard player named Mike Michaels—a vending machine operator by day and wannabe actor/mafioso by night. He spoke almost exclusively in Joe Pesci references, often prefaced by "Bro Bro." The female singer was a pretty girl who sang well enough, while the drummer worked as an insurance salesman by day. I was the only person in this band with ambition to take it further, while they remained perfectly content with a couple of gigs a month and a little pocket change. Despite this, because it was the first working band I'd ever been in, I was thoroughly excited to set the musical world on fire. I earnestly learned their whole set of songs, including their versions of "I Will Survive," "Oye Como Va," "December 1963 (Oh, What a Night)," and "Copacabana," to name a few.

I was told that we'd start with some smaller gigs to tighten up the band and springboard us into the big-time, A-list rooms and lucrative wedding scene, as Mike Michaels was "well-connected." Wow, it was all happening so quickly—my first real band, and already I was hitting the big time.

These "starter" gigs, however, turned out to be the only gigs we ever played. We had a regular stint at a Holiday Inn lounge in Clarke, NJ, highlighted by a once-a-month gathering of the local swingers club. The music was cheesy, and the atmosphere was as depressing as you might expect. But I didn't know any better, and I could finally call myself a "professional musician."

I was beginning to learn my craft, including a basic repertoire of songs. The only problem (as I'd later learn) was that Mike Michaels played every song in the key of C, regardless of whether it was supposed to be. Every. Single. Song. "Wind Beneath My Wings" in C, "Get Down Tonight" in C, "Copacabana"—you guessed it, C.

Later, when I played those same songs in other bands, I thought I was prepared. I was not. The singers grimaced, the band sounded off, and I was that wide-eyed kid who had no idea what was happening. It didn't take long for me to figure out that I needed to relearn every song in its proper key—and fast. Nights were spent transposing, memorizing, and practicing, trying to get it right before the next show. Soon, I could transpose on the fly, and those gigs became a real-world boot camp in musicianship you couldn't get in school.

I played in Super Fresh for about two years before it fizzled out. I was already on the hunt for new opportunities to play with different musicians—and other keys. [Side note: Not long after this, I would hire a reunited Super Fresh to play at my wedding.]

Have Guitar, Will Pay Parking Tickets

In my attempt to become a freelance guitar player, I began playing with some singer-songwriters in New York City, hoping one of them would be my ticket to success. I thought of it like playing the lottery. Eventually, one of them could be the winning ticket to the big time.

But I quickly learned that the lifespan of a New York singer/songwriter was often quite short. Playing original music of any kind is always a challenge, and the economics aren't in your favor, especially in a hub like New York, where there is so much competition.

If you want your songs to be heard, you need to hire musicians and studios to record them. To play your songs live and be seen, you'd have to play these showcase gigs where four to six bands would play per night, each getting about 45 minutes. The songwriter would make next to nothing unless they could bring in a big crowd. They still had to pay their band and do whatever amount of publicity they could muster.

Unless they could excite audiences and build a strong following, these gigs always resulted in a financial loss, and most of the artists I accompanied didn't last long.

I performed with several of these hopefuls, and loved playing their original music. Learning how to use my musical personality to interpret someone else's artistic vision was a challenge. Still, I got pretty good at dialing back my own style and playing what the song needed for the people who wrote it. I made a lot of mistakes early on trying to be too clever and overplaying, until I was once admonished by a country/rock singer I played with:

"Take it easy there, fella. We don't wanna hear none of those faggot jazz chords." (*His words, not mine.*)

Message received.

I loved the different styles of music I got to play during this period and had always thought of myself as a rocker at heart. I learned otherwise. I spent many years in a band with a rock singer, Christine Martucci, who is well-known around New Jersey. She's an original artist, a hard-rocking chick in the vein of Melissa Etheridge or Janis Joplin. I had the opportunity to play some great gigs with her, including at the legendary Stone Pony in Asbury Park, New Jersey, on several occasions.

My time in her band gave me an introduction to what it's like being in a *real* rock band. Her drummer at the time was already a friend of mine and is a very lovable guy. He's the embodiment of New Jersey: loud, funny, crude, and fueled by Jack Daniels. He always made everyone laugh.

One perk of playing gigs is that there is plenty of booze around, and some people take full advantage of that. That was never my style. Don't get me wrong,

I like to "hydrate" as much as the next guy, but not until *after* the gig is over and I've done my job.

Suffice it to say, this band could drink, and not just at gigs. They drank at *rehearsals*. Even though I had gained a reputation in musical circles as being a "jazz guy," I held the illusion that I could rock with the best of them. Apparently, I wasn't there yet. As I politely sipped on a glass of wine, my friend would push a bottle of whiskey into my chest and say, "Put down that pansy shit and drink some of this." I'll admit, I indulged on those gigs more than I ever had or would afterward, but hey, when in Rome.

Postscript: My drummer friend would later go to rehab and quit drinking for good.

As much as those experiences helped season me as a freelance guitarist—like musical Navy SEAL training without the push-ups—I ultimately stopped doing them. I might've earned $50, but after gas, tolls, and the privilege of donating half my pay to the New York Department of Transportation for parking, I'd end up with next to nothing.

We might've also been the fourth band in the night's lineup, but things always ran late, which meant sitting through two bands who gave us a lesson in how *not* to play music. When it was finally our turn, we'd have to quickly throw our gear on stage, perform the shortest soundcheck ever, and then give our audience of five everything we had.

But once we actually started playing, I loved it—the music, the energy, the people. I met some great musicians during those nights, with whom I still play today. Still, everything surrounding those gigs began to make me face an undeniable realization: I learned a lot musically, but my parking ticket collection was growing faster than my bank account.

It was around that time that I began having my first brushes with musical fame—always followed by a reminder that I wasn't there. One prime example came backstage at a music festival where I was performing with a local singer. While hanging out in the hospitality tent, I stumbled upon Levon Helm, the iconic drummer and singer for The Band. Nervous and excited, I reached out my hand and said, "It's a real pleasure to meet you, Mr. Helm." He extended his hand to meet mine—and that's when the joint that had been in his mouth dropped to the ground between us. He looked mildly annoyed. That was our conversation. I felt terrible. First impressions have never been my strong suit.

That handshake has typified my career—so close to musical glory, yet somehow turning every near-success into a story worth laughing about later.

Opening Measures

And this was all just the beginning—more music, more gigs, and countless adventures lay ahead. Sometimes I got it right; sometimes I didn't. Either way, that's how I stumbled and strummed my way into the music scene. A few wrong turns, a few right notes, and many stories later, I'm still doing what that 13-year-old bass player dreamed of: making music, one (occasionally weird) gig at a time.

3

Sing, Sing, Sing

Early on, while I was keeping busy as a guitarist-for-hire, I also started running my own bands. They were instrumental jazz groups, and—as I'll get into later—we played everywhere: restaurants, cocktail parties, coffeehouses, you name it.

But in 2005, a couple hired us to play at their wedding. On the surface, this was no big deal; we'd played plenty of those before. But we'd always been hired to play during the cocktail hour or to provide some nice dinner music, accompanied by polite claps from the antipasto station, before the DJ or wedding band escalated it into party mode—the human equivalent of a Spotify "Chill Vibes" playlist. This time, the groom-to-be threw me a curveball.

He asked, "Can you guys add a singer?" Huh. I'd never been asked that before. It's not that we *couldn't* do it; we just hadn't. But one thing I've learned about hustling up work is never to say no. If someone asked, "Can you guys play Lithuanian folk music?" I'd say, "Of course we can," then figure it out after booking the gig. If they asked, "Can you bring someone to play a didgeridoo in your band?" I'd say, "Of course I can. We do it all the time," then google "What is a didgeridoo?"

So, do we play with a singer? Of *course* we do! Total bluff.

I was already familiar with a decent amount of that repertoire from playing in other bands, and I figured my guys were good enough to easily put something together. But first, I needed a singer.

I asked around and was recommended a guy named Justin Wade. I called Justin and told him we needed a singer for a wedding, and he courageously (or foolishly) agreed. I also warned him that there weren't going to be any rehearsals; we would just show up and "wing it" (which is a "normal night" for a jazz ensemble). Of course, I'd prepared a list of songs and written some of the music out so we'd all be on the same page. Still, it was new territory to run a band this way, and we were going to have to fly by the seat of our pants.

We arrived at the venue—a train station in Philadelphia. Its unique character and superb acoustics made it quite the romantic backdrop—unless you've been involved in an Amtrak disaster of any sort. I met Justin about 10 minutes before it was time to start, and he was undoubtedly as nervous as I was. Ruining someone's wedding isn't a good career move.

But we stuck to the plan, played through the list, and it went off without a hitch. The groom even told us we were the best wedding band he'd ever heard! It made me wonder how many weddings he'd been to, but, hey, if that's what he thought, who was I to argue?

At that gig, the "B.D. Lenz All Stars" was born (not the most creative band name, I admit, but I was going for easy, not clever). Justin was now the singer of my new vocal band, which would run parallel with my jazz group but be a much better earner. We would go on to play all kinds of gigs, including the biggest paydays: weddings. The vocal band was never as busy as my jazz group because it wasn't my primary focus. Still, it's opened numerous opportunities for me to work and connect with other great musicians I've hired to play in it.

After a couple of years of working in this configuration, a young woman called me to find a band for her upcoming wedding. Coincidentally, she lived in my neighborhood, and I encouraged her to come see us play a local gig sometime. As luck would have it, we had one just a few weeks later. She said she would go, but also asked if it would be possible to get up and sing a song with us. As I mentioned earlier, it's not uncommon for someone to ask to "sit in" with us during gigs. I try to be gracious and usually say yes, but it doesn't always go well, and there's always the risk of an absolute embarrassment for everyone involved. Still, I wanted to book this wedding, so I agreed.

A few songs into our set, a young woman walked in with her mother, and I knew immediately she was the bride-to-be I'd been speaking with. During the next break, I introduced myself and invited her to come up and sing the song we had agreed on: "Crazy," by Gnarls Barkley. She seemed a bit unsure at first, and I braced for the worst. But as she began singing, I realized that she was good. Like, really good! As we got further into the song and she loosened up, I was actually blown away. What a pleasant surprise—she crushed it.

Afterward, we chatted a bit, and the coincidences continued. It turned out that this future bride was an aspiring singer and had recently recorded an album on which I had played! I hadn't met her because she wasn't at that recording session. Needless to say, I booked her wedding.

In preparation for her big day, she wanted to write a song dedicated to her father to sing at the reception, so we wrote one together. The song was called "Daddy Did You Know," and it was a heartfelt tearjerker. Only he didn't cry. Nevertheless, it began a working relationship that has lasted to this day.

Not long after, Lelica Palecco joined the B.D. Lenz All Stars to share vocal duties with Justin, and we would go on to co-write and record two albums of her original music. She was initially inexperienced with the mechanics of playing gigs but would later blossom into a great musician, bandleader, and songwriter in her own right.

And the Crowd Goes Mild

She was the last piece of the puzzle missing from my band. With the addition of a female voice, we now had a much wider repertoire, and the B.D. Lenz All Stars was officially complete.

As the band got busier, not every member was available for every gig, so I've had to find backups for everyone. I've built up quite the roster of subs for every instrument, and at this point, could probably staff a whole music festival just from my backup list.

In simplest terms, this band is a cover band, but at the same time, I never wanted it to be a "cover band." What I mean is, I didn't want to play the same clubs where typical cover bands play. I'd rather work higher-end private events that pay much better and don't always require catering to a specific audience's tastes. I never wanted to keep up with the latest radio hits or be relegated to churning out the played-out oldies.

We play a wide variety of genres, including Motown, funk, rock, reggae, pop, and jazz. But I think we're better defined by the songs we *don't* play rather than the ones we do: "Jessie's Girl," "Livin' On a Prayer," "Brown Eyed Girl," and "Sweet Caroline." Those won't be on our setlist. No offense to Neil Diamond, but I never want to have to shout "So good! So good! So good!" ever again. They're classics for sure, but they're only fun the first 10,000 times you play them. Oh, and we *don't* play line dances!

We also don't play with backing tracks, matching outfits, synchronized dance moves, glow sticks, inflatable saxophones, or sequins. No shtick, just great musicians playing great songs.

However, we need to be flexible to suit any situation. Many venues can't handle a full band, so we can easily scale down to a four-piece or even an acoustic duo, if necessary. On the other hand, some clients want a larger band, so we'll add keyboards or even a horn section, depending on their preferences. Adaptability keeps the phone ringing.

It's comical how often I end up booking gigs for this band when the client's original intention was seemingly to book my jazz group. The conversations typically go like this:

Client: "Hey there. I'm interested in booking your jazz group for an event."
Me: "Ok, great. Do you know how big a band or what instruments you'd like?"
Client: "Not exactly, but can you bring a singer?"
Me: "Sure, we can do that. So you want a *jazz* singer?"
Client: "Yes, but can they sing songs people know?"
Me: "Yes, of course. Do you mean jazz standards that people know?"
Client: "Well…you know…more current stuff."
Me: "Ok, so you *don't* want a jazz group? You want something more current?"
Client: "Yes, something people can dance to."
Me: "Ok, got it. I have just the band for that."

I have that exchange all the time. It turns out they didn't want Billie Holiday; they wanted Billie Eilish.

The world of cover bands is highly competitive, especially when it comes to booking weddings, where the biggest money is at stake. You must be committed to working in that world, as you're constantly learning

And the Crowd Goes Mild

the latest hits and have to play free "showcases" for potential couples. Most bands that frequently play weddings have a splashy demo video and might even work for an agency that also books several other groups. Those bands usually have generic names such as "Hit Patrol" or "Electric Boulevard."

I've subbed in these kinds of ensembles and found them a bit soulless and impersonal. The musicians can be excellent, but they're constantly rotating in and out, as they're often mercenaries just making money between tours or other gigs. I never wanted my band to be like these. As much as I've been accused of being a "gig whore," I still need some connection to the music and the people I play it with. I'd rather play fewer gigs than feel like a migrant worker in a wedding band sweatshop. There's no artistic value in them, just decent money and maybe a good time, which is fine for many, but not for me.

I once was called to substitute in a 10-piece wedding band that worked for such an agency. I didn't know anyone else in this group, but that didn't bother me. They sent me their song list in advance, and I arrived well-prepared. The first set was cocktail-hour jazz—pleasant, relaxed, and uneventful. When we finished the set, the musicians began walking off the bandstand, and I was excited to help myself to the scraps from the leftover hors d'oeuvres; I was starving. But as I began taking my guitar off my shoulders, the bandleader walked over to me and said, "Hey man, I'm going to need you to stay on stage and play solo during this set break." I felt a jolt of irritation streak through my body.

My head was swirling with questions like "Huh? Why? Why *me*?" but my mouth simply croaked, "Uh. Ok." He sprang that tidbit on me right then, and I was left utterly confused. After everyone else had left the stage, I stood there by myself, playing instrumental guitar. I watched the rest of the band at the far end of the room eating beef sliders, sipping on wine, and raising their glasses towards me with a "cheers" to let me know I was doing alright. Inside, I was fuming and had so many questions. Why was I there by myself? They'd never met me, so how did they even know that I could play solo? Why did they get to stand there eating crab cakes while I was on stage playing "The Girl From Ipanema?"

I found out later that their agency advertises "continuous music." Somebody had to be playing at all times. The next set break was the piano player's turn, but I missed out on some good grub. "Continuous music" to me meant *continuous hunger*. Thanks for the heads up, guys.

Having my *own* vocal band finally gave me a solid answer to the eternal question, "So… where's your singer?" It also came with a surprising bonus: turns out melodies with lyrics are better for the bank account. The downside? It's also landed me in some hilariously uncomfortable situations—stories I'll gladly share for your entertainment.

4

Send in the Clowns

I've used the word *gig* quite a bit. It's a wonderfully vague term born from jazz musicians in the 1920s. It can refer to anything from a major concert to a dimly lit club date—or simply playing unobtrusively while guests work their way through shrimp cocktail at a corporate mixer. Generally, it implies that the band is getting paid, though not necessarily enough to mention on a tax return or in polite conversation.

Over the years, I've played a staggering variety of them in an equally strange assortment of places. Sure, I've worked all the usual venues you'd expect: bars, festivals, cafes, and theaters.

But then there are the others—the ones you'd never think of as a setting to inspire music. Furniture stores.

Grocery stores (the puzzled looks on people's faces as they left the register were priceless). Car dealerships. Corporate cubicles. Aquariums. Museums. Liquor stores. Medical offices. Cigar lounges (great crowds if you don't mind the coughing). Department stores. You name it.

If there's an electrical outlet, I've probably set up an amp there. They're not always places to create art—just do a job and not block the fire exit.

I should take this moment to brag a little. I ought to mention that if you ever see the legendary Apollo Theater in Harlem, New York, I've had the honor of performing there. Well... let me clarify. Just to the *left* of the Apollo, adjacent to it, is a Blick Art Materials store, and that's where I played—at their grand opening, somewhere between the glue sticks and the coloring books. Still, whenever a picture of the Apollo pops up, and even one pixel of that art store sneaks into the frame, I proudly tell people, "Yep. I've played there."

That pretty much sums up life as a working musician: close enough to greatness to see it, far enough away to be reminded we're not on the guest list.

There's never been an occasion too small or too grand: weddings, birthdays, graduations, anniversaries, and store grand openings. Basically, any occasion where people gather to celebrate, often with cake and sometimes with a drink being spilled on my amplifier.

It's nice when your place of work is a festive occasion. Guests are usually cheerful, and clients are generous about keeping the band watered and fed (although it's not a good idea to eat *too* much before the second set). But you get numb to the cheer after a while, as we're really just there to work.

Clients will sometimes encourage us to party right along with them, lining up shots and feeding us cocktails; after all, we *are* the band. It's flattering, but I still have to drive home.

Then, there are the hundreds upon hundreds of corporate galas, conferences, exhibitions, and retreats I've serenaded. I've listened to way too many sales presentations and CEO speeches, all while my bandmates and I quietly exchanged immature jokes, feeling like a pack of mischievous teenagers at the back of the class—except for the small fact that we're all members of AARP. If you've never sat through a motivational sales PowerPoint while trying not to snort-laugh at your drummer's running under-his-breath commentary, consider yourself lucky.

Private events typically pay the best and come in all shapes and levels of strangeness. They're often in people's homes, and I've played at some massive properties for some exceptionally wealthy people. The Instagram pictures look amazing and would lead you to believe we're part of that world, but the hard truth is, we're only hired help, one step above the catering staff.

Take, for instance, the time I was called to be part of a jazz quartet performing in someone's backyard. It turned out that "backyard" was a compound in Greenwich, Connecticut. If you don't know Greenwich, that's where money hires a financial advisor to manage its other financial advisors. It's one of the wealthiest zip codes in the country.

I was told to show up in a tuxedo, which made me imagine it to be a lavish soirée à la "The Great Gatsby." Not exactly. Instead, we found ourselves playing next to a pool while a family of five swam and grilled burgers. That was it. No party, no guests. Just one very rich family who decided a live jazz quartet was the perfect soundtrack for floating on pool noodles and eating barbecue on a Thursday afternoon. I'd never played guitar solos behind "Marco…Polo…" and haven't since.

It's incredible how accustomed I've become to showing up at new places, setting up in front of a group of strangers and playing my guitar. Only when I step outside of myself do I recognize how odd the whole thing can be.

Like the time a woman hired me to play solo guitar while she cooked dinner for her boyfriend's birthday. It sounded sweet until I realized it was *just the two of them…and me*. They dined, they looked lovingly into each other's eyes, they exchanged sweet nothings, all while I sat three feet away, pretending not to notice a thing.

It was just another gig with another audience. I've never stared at my shoes so intently while trying to concentrate on the chords to "Misty." They were actually a lovely couple, and thankfully, things never got *too* uncomfortable, but I left feeling like I had been an extra in a bad rom-com.

And the Crowd Goes Mild

I've been good at getting gigs, and I've always worked a lot. But early on, I chose quantity over quality. Yeah, some were downright...unusual. My bandmates jokingly dubbed our experience the "B.D. Lenz Theater of the Bizarre." When you show up to work with me, you never know what you're in for; it could be cool, or it could be weird. (Or both!)

But an unspoken rule in this line of work is, you don't say no. I was given sage advice early on: Don't turn down a gig unless it fails to meet at least one of the following three criteria: good money, good music, or good musicians. If you're fortunate, you'll get all three. But typically, it's one and a funny story. The amount of money that makes a gig "worth it" is different for everyone and often changes over time, but I've rarely turned down work I was grateful to get.

I began booking my own gigs after college in the late '90s, just as the internet was starting to take off. Hungry for work, I dove into this new digital frontier and the new wave of online booking sites that were emerging to book live entertainment. Bands could post digital press kits—photos, videos, reviews—and clients could browse and hire acts directly. It was simple, straightforward, and utterly revolutionary at the time.

I signed up early and with remarkable success. As the platforms grew, so did my calendar. They quickly became the go-to way to find bands, much like people use the internet today to find any product or service. I booked countless gigs, providing steady work at a time when I had no connections or established reputation. What did people even do before the internet? But I digress.

When I book a gig online, I rarely meet the client before the event. Occasionally, I might speak with them on the phone, but most of the time, communication is limited to email. That can make it tricky to get a sense of who your customer is, leaving you to walk into situations a bit blind.

I'll share with you the perfect example. On one occasion, we were booked to play at a Halloween party at a beautiful mansion in Westchester, New York. The host requested costumes, so I phoned it in with my usual Gilligan outfit—white hat, red shirt, the whole deal. While setting up, we were greeted by the woman who'd hired us—she was friendly and welcoming. But when her husband came downstairs and saw a band erecting a P.A. system in his living room, he lost his mind. Apparently, he never got the memo. He demanded to know why we were there and who booked us (ummm, your wife?). We froze, unsure of what to do next. His wife tried to smooth things over by explaining that he "doesn't like surprises." After a loud "discussion" in another room, he returned much calmer, let us play, and by the end of the night, even liked us. I filed this under "success," but only because I don't have a manila folder labeled "trauma."

Boats, however, are a category unto themselves. Living near New York City, I've worked on a surprising number of them. Cruising around Manhattan and up the Hudson River is a beautiful, scenic trip I never get tired of—gorgeous skyline, fresh breeze, and a front-row view of Lady Liberty herself. These trips are popular for celebrations where people might indulge in a cocktail of champagne and Dramamine. Nothing says refinement like jazz and seasickness.

For a while, I even subbed on a high-end dinner cruise that circled New York Harbor nightly. After a few runs, I was able to master the "power stance"—the wide-legged pose guitarists use when they look like they're about to unleash rock fury—but in this case, it was simply to stay upright while the boat swayed over rough waters. Real "yacht rock," in every sense.

While the anecdotes I shared earlier were awkward, they had happy endings—they don't *always* end that way. Let's get to the downright bad ones, the stories we tell over drinks. We can laugh now, but they weren't funny at the time. Time and therapy have ripened these sour grapes into sweet, hilarious wine. Let's start with one that took place on one of those boats.

Batten down the hatches, there's rough seas ahead.

Sailing the S.S. Regret

I was contacted through one of the online booking sites to play at an after-party for a formal event hosted by a Princeton University "eating club" (their co-ed version of a fraternity or sorority). These students would attend their gala in Princeton, then hop a bus to New York City to party on a boat cruising around Manhattan—serenaded by yours truly.

This sounded like it would be super posh: Princeton University, Manhattan cruise, a truly Ivy League experience. I was expecting a good payday and a lot of fun. (Spoiler alert: It was neither.)

I had just started playing with a renowned local drummer named Abe Fogle. Abe has played with a laundry list of famous artists, including Kool and the Gang, D'Angelo, Gavin DeGraw, and Roger Waters. In fact, he had just gotten off a tour playing arenas with Rob Thomas (of Matchbox 20 fame), and I was hiring him to play with me, hoping to make a connection with this tremendous talent.

We arrived at the Manhattan pier at a suspiciously late hour. It was dark, deserted, and so foggy that the vessel at the end of a dock was barely visible.

We loaded our gear onto a large dolly and began rolling it towards the boat. The P.A. system, guitar amps, and drum kit were precariously perched while we moved as slowly and cautiously as possible, barely able to see five feet in front of us. In the eerie quiet, the only noise was the creaky planks beneath our feet, until suddenly...*SPLASH!*

My stomach sank. *What was that? Was that my guitar? Please, don't be Abe's drums or I'll owe him money and he'll never want to play with me again.*

Panicked, we shone our phones over the water, searching for whatever had chosen to "abandon ship." After a tense minute, I spotted it: a black bag briefly floating on the surface before sinking below, leaving only a gurgle of bubbles in its wake. This was a textbook case of good news, bad news—the good news: It wasn't a piece of Abe's drum kit. The bad news: It was the bag that contained all the cables and microphones for my P.A. system. Gone. The Hudson River was now equipped for its own underwater open-mic night.

I was already deflated, and we hadn't even played a single note. Not only would it be expensive to replace all that equipment, but a more pressing issue was how my singer, Justin, would sing without a microphone or speaker cables. We'd have to figure that out later.

In the meantime, we got the rest of the gear to the boat, and as it began revealing itself through the fog, I was shocked by what I saw. I was expecting a beautiful, luxurious yacht. Instead, we were greeted by a small, rickety old heap that looked like it had sailed through three hurricanes. It was so dilapidated even pirates would've considered it a liability. I expected more from Princeton kids. I bet Harvard brats would've had a fully staffed schooner with Wi-Fi, a string quartet, and someone taking attendance for their future Supreme Court clerkship.

We were told to set up in the main cabin, but it was so small that it could barely fit the four of us and our gear. Abe couldn't even fit his drum stool; he sat on the metal bench lining the cabin's interior.

But there was a big problem: We still had no P.A. The captain came to the rescue with an old microphone, which he plugged into the boat's speaker system. It sounded terrible, like a New York Subway public address system, but it was all we had, and we had to go with it.

"Attention passengers: Here's a short safety announcement. Life jackets are available... somewhere. If you find one, don't tell anyone."

Once set up, the Princeton kids arrived in their formal wear—time to plaster on a fake smile and make the best of it. Like the professionals we are, we launched right into our party favorites, hoping to lift everyone's spirits, including our own.

"Hate" might be too strong a word—I wouldn't say they *hated* us. "Indifferent" might be a more accurate description. These collegiates barely even acknowledged we were there. They clearly didn't enjoy it, and, consequently, neither did we. So there we were, jam-packed into this tiny, derelict, dimly lit boat on a night as dreary as my soul was. Justin was singing through the boat speaker, which sounded like he was announcing the next stop on the F train. I had lost a bag of pricey equipment, and our audience was miserable. *Why do I do this again?*

I counted the minutes until the ordeal was over. It was one of those nights that made me want to go home, crawl into bed, and start over again the next day.

When the end mercifully came, we began packing up (I wasn't sure the kids even noticed), and the young man who hired us approached me with an envelope of cash to settle up. Inside was an extra $100—a tip. It was a genuinely kind gesture and helped tamp down some of the bitterness. Like a good bandleader, I paid everyone their usual rate, plus an extra $25 each—a small silver lining.

The next morning, as I attempted to shake off the discouragement and regain my positivity, I got a call from the kid who had booked us:

Kid: "Hey, did you notice an extra $100 in the envelope last night?"
Me: "I did. That was very generous. Thank you."
Kid: "Yeah, ummm, that was a mistake. I didn't mean to give that to you. Could you send that back?"

Oof. Yeah, I returned it, knowing deep down that someday that guy would be a hedge fund manager, and I didn't want him coming after me for compound interest.

Speaking of interest, here's one about a holiday party that nearly made me lose *all* interest in ever playing music again.

Oh Come All Ye Painful

Ah, the holidays. A time of year filled with good cheer and merriment. It's always a busy and lucrative time for working musicians. There's a lot of "rocking around the Christmas tree," but some gigs can be less "joy to the world" and more "everybody hurts sometimes," as I'll share with you.

My tale begins with a woman from a country club in northern New Jersey contacting me to play at their annual Christmas party. They wanted my vocal band to play a nice mix that included some holiday classics. Simple enough, right?

We arrived, upbeat and ready to spread some festive cheer, when the club president (the woman's husband) asked to say a few words. They were short remarks with the usual pleasantries, but I'll never forget the closing line: "It's nice to be among like-minded people who can get together and enjoy each other's company." It seemed cringy to me, even at the time, as my brain translated it to: "Welcome to a room full of rich people who all agree to be just as insufferable." But the true irony of his words would reveal itself later.

We began the night with a few holiday songs, and the crowd seemed pleasant enough as they settled in with food and drinks. During the second song, however, an older gentleman walked over to me and requested a song that I didn't recognize. I politely replied, "I'm sorry, sir, I'm not familiar with that one," to which he immediately asked for another.

Again, it was probably some rare B-side from 1962, and I didn't know it. He looked stunned, his face showing a look of pure disgust, as if I'd suggested replacing his eggnog with a kale smoothie.

I've been playing music professionally for decades. Obviously, there are many songs I don't know; there are thousands upon thousands, after all. But on most nights, I can accommodate a good percentage of the songs people usually request. Well, not that night, and he didn't take it well.

"Well, what *do* you know?" he snapped.

How could I even answer that? "Ummm… I have a song list I could show you," I replied apologetically,

And the Crowd Goes Mild

but before I even finished speaking, he had already stormed off and sat down indignantly. I felt bad we couldn't honor his requests—but honestly, his reaction was rude.

No more than five minutes later, while in the middle of the next song, an older woman shuffled up to me and said, "I don't like this song, could you play something else?"

I was stunned. Nobody had ever said that to me before. I'm not suggesting that everyone should like every song we play; they can't all be your favorites. But we're not going to stop in the middle of one to change it just for one person. What happened to "Tis the season to be jolly"?

Once again, I tried to keep my cool. "I'm sorry, ma'am, but I hope you'll like the next one." (I'm sure she didn't like *any* of them, or life itself, for that matter.)

Fast forward a few minutes, and the woman who hired us charged over to me and grumbled, "It's getting too loud, could you please turn it down?"

Remember my list of common complainers in chapter 1? They all showed up together at this party. It truly was the most miserable group of people I'd ever encountered. The parade of discontent only continued throughout the rest of the first set and into the second. Seriously, we might get one or two of those on a typical night, but this was a steady procession of "Karens" who "wanted to speak to the manager" of music, which, unfortunately, happened to be me. They all felt the need to express their

59

distaste about something we were, or were not, playing. I tried gritting my teeth and reminding myself that I'd never have to see them again.

But wait—this gingerbread house was only *beginning* to crumble.

A significant portion of the audience was older, in their sixties and beyond; however, there was also a group of younger women sitting together at a table right next to us. I would estimate their ages to have been in their late thirties to early forties, but they were easily twenty years younger than their husbands, who were smoking cigars in the back of the room. The amount of plastic among this group of women was as toxic as their level of entitlement, and the drunker they got, the more vocal they became about their dislike of our song selections. They disapproved of the songs we were playing to make the older crowd happy (even though we weren't even managing to do that).

They began heckling us and demanding something they could dance to. Yes, they were actually *heckling* us. That doesn't happen either. I've played for rude, pushy people, but I've never been outright heckled or jeered at. The ringleader even began pointing at my singer and saying nasty things to her to make us comply. It was rising to a new level of ugliness that I had never experienced before.

After being bullied into submission by the younger contingent, we relented, shifted gears, and launched into our party set—complete with dance-floor staples. Miraculously, it worked…for all of three minutes. They danced briefly, then resumed complaining.

Not long into that set, the woman who'd hired us marched back over, insisting we *turn it down*. After all, her guests wanted soft music. I explained—politely but with the spiritual energy of a man unraveling—that others had just begged for something to dance to. It didn't seem to register with her.

She stomped away, only to be followed by her husband, who angrily demanded that we *turn it down, immediately*. I'd never been yelled at like that on a gig. That was the moment I reached peak despair. It was "Do They Know It's Christmas?" when all I wanted was "Silent Night."

After we finished the song, we turned it back down again and played something quieter. But it only upset the drunk trophy wives even more—they still wanted to dance.

I was caught in a full-blown musical tug-of-war and felt utterly helpless. I couldn't choose songs anymore—there were two completely different camps in attendance and pleasing one instantly infuriated the other. As the bandleader, I was supposed to steer the ship by picking songs, but I'd hit my limit and mentally checked out. Fortunately, my bandmates stepped in and took over, with the same lack of success.

Remember the line about *"like-minded people?"* Hilarious.

Slowly, the guests began to leave early, presumably seeking refuge from the musical apocalypse that had occurred. I wish we could have left, too. Still, as professionals, we played until the bitter end. (This experience helped me find spiritual oneness with the band that played on the deck of the Titanic as it sank into the icy Atlantic.)

All we wanted to do was help these folks have an enjoyable evening, but it wasn't meant to be. Nobody had an enjoyable evening. Never before, or since, have I experienced that level of rudeness, entitlement, and saltiness. Happy Holidays!

Now, I know, every job has bad days, and I am mindful that mine would never compare to those of, say, a surgeon or a pilot. Bad guitar playing hasn't ever killed anyone or forced a jumbo jet to go down in flames (yet). The worst I'd done was to make a few rich people mildly furious, turn holiday cheer into a lump of coal, and force my singer to reevaluate her career choice. Yup, perspective is key.

How about one more? At this point, I could use one with a *happy* ending…and a glass of merlot.

Late to the Party

Punctuality is mandatory in most professions, and musicians are supposed to act like professionals. I've heard it said, "If you're not early, you're late." But clearly, whoever said that has never driven to Long Island, New York.

And the Crowd Goes Mild

If you're not familiar with the New York area, let me enlighten you on what it's like to drive to this "Island of Long." Imagine receiving a thousand razor blade cuts to your body, then being gently dipped into a vat of artisanal sea salt. I might be exaggerating, but only by a little. I've come to hate that drive. The trip could take one hour—or five—to go to the same place, but rest assured, traffic is going to be terrible. There are only a few bridges to the island, and they're always congested. Then, once you get on the Long Island Expressway, it will ruin your day.

A groom once hired my band to play at his wedding in Long Island. A few days before the big day, he called to ask what time I planned to leave to make the 6pm start time. I said 3pm. He was not happy and reacted as if I told him I was planning to arrive from space using only the power of positive thinking. He told me it wasn't early enough and we'd better get there on time. I mean, yeah, he was right—it was one of the most important days of his life, and I was responsible for being there on time. But I also didn't think it required me to leave at sunrise as though I was driving a covered wagon across the plains.

My band was carpooling together from New Jersey, and, naturally, we hit brutal traffic. As the GPS continued to recalculate, it became apparent that our ETA would be 6pm on the dot. I was getting panicked. *Arriving* at 6pm wasn't enough time to be set up and ready to play as per the contract. The groom even called mid-drive to check that we were en route, and I assured him we were while secretly wondering whether being "fashionably late" only applied to social events.

Knowing I'll be late to a gig is the worst feeling in the world, especially in the case of a wedding. I hoped I didn't become this couple's cautionary tale about booking bands from New Jersey.

I was slated to play the ceremony solo, before the rest of the band joined in for the cocktail hour and reception. So, while on the way, we devised a plan. When we arrived at the venue, I would grab my guitar and amp, jump out of the car, sprint to where the ceremony was being held, and quickly set up, *praying* that the groom hadn't seen me parkour over a hedge. At the same time, the rest of the band would park the car and set up the rest of the gear in the reception area, where I would rejoin them later.

We arrived *right* at 6pm and put our plan into motion. Completely frantic, I jumped out of the car, grabbed my stuff, climbed over a fence, and ran to the outdoor space where I was supposed to be playing the ceremony. But when I got there, out of breath and sweaty, I was bewildered to find nobody else there. I was sure I was in the right place. Regardless, I plugged in, sat down, and began warming up, pretending I had been there for ages.

A few minutes later, the groom walked over, looking miffed. Oh boy, here it comes—I braced for a verbal smackdown.

"Hey there. Where is everyone?" I asked, pretending to be calm, relaxed, and *not* completely out of breath.

His reply was vindication that filled my soul. "You're actually the first one here."

"What?" I asked, pretending to be concerned, but secretly high-fiving myself.

"Yeah. Apparently, the traffic is so bad that everyone is still on the way. The guests, the staff, and even the officiant won't be here for another hour."

If words were a person, I would've kissed them. Sure, I was technically late. But spiritually? Emotionally? I'd already written my acceptance speech for Most Professional Musician of the Year. Not to brag, but for one hour, I was the most punctual guitarist in Nassau County.

The moral of this story? I guess it's that "on time" is subjective, and so is my ability to estimate traffic.

From Living Room to Barroom

I've shared stories about playing private gigs—and if private gigs are music school homework, public shows are the pop quiz you weren't ready for. In public venues, like bars or clubs, anything can happen, and usually does. Like how to smile through feedback, play through the sound of someone vomiting next to the stage, or look appreciative when someone says, "Don't you guys know anything good?"

Step onto a public stage, and anything can happen. I've played in bars where the vibe was electric—crowds singing along, bartenders dancing, everyone caught up in the moment. And I've played others where the only people paying attention were the ones waiting for us to stop so they could hear the game.

I've lost count of how many times I've been in the middle of a guitar solo, eyes closed, pouring my heart into it, when huge applause erupted. For a split second, I'd think, *Yes! They felt it—I've really reached these people,* only to open my eyes and realize that everyone was cheering at the TV as Aaron Judge rounded the bases. That's...humbling.

I've even played gigs where people were genuinely upset that we had the nerve to perform during a big game. Case in point was the time a band I was in got booked to play during the Super Bowl.

The Super Bowl? Who the hell thought it was a good idea to book a live band opposite the biggest televised event in America? The gig was at a casino (talk about an odd mix of humanity), and do you think any of those people wanted to hear us? (Spoiler alert: They would have been happier to listen to the sound of someone hitting triple sevens.) The only way they would have liked us was if we'd intercepted a pass.

Heck, even *we* were watching the game while going through the motions of playing our set. The singer, a Philadelphia Eagles fan, randomly inserted "Fly Eagles fly" into songs as he cheered his team on. I remember playing a Steve Miller classic especially for this event: "I want to fly like an eagle, to the sea. Fly like an eagle, let my spirit carry me..."

I've come to realize there are two kinds of gigs. Sometimes, you're there to create something meaningful. Others, you're there just to fill the space with sound.

And the Crowd Goes Mild

At its best, playing music is magic. You get lost in a moment of creativity and feel connected to something bigger than yourself. At its worst, you can feel like a dancing bear or a juggling clown, beholden to whoever has rented you for the evening. Sometimes, instead of being part of the experience, you become the thing interrupting it. I've felt all of this, sometimes within the same night.

But the trick isn't judging—being professional means knowing which kind it is before expecting more from the room than it ever planned to give. Either way, I show up early, say yes, play through whatever comes, smile like it's going great, and never take anything personally. That's what's kept the "B.D. Lenz Theater of the Bizarre" in business all these years.

5

A Day in the Life

What people imagine a musician's life to be and what it actually is are about as similar as a red herring and Red Lobster. From the outside, all anyone sees is what happens onstage and the carefully curated, "living the dream" Instagram posts. What remains invisible are the countless tasks required before a single note is played—the spreadsheets, emails, invoices, and, yes, all the practicing that make the whole thing possible. The music itself is usually the fun part. But it represents only the tip of the proverbial iceberg. Below the surface lies a much larger—and far more boring—chunk of iceberg.

Let's talk about the mundane realities you probably never imagined an "artist type" would have to deal with offstage.

The "Busyness" in the Music Business

There's always some amount of music-related busywork to attend to during the day. You might think I just roll up to gigs, play some tunes, get paid, and then float home on a cloud of applause. I wish.

Behind every gig is a pile of admin that makes me feel less like a free-spirited musician and more like an office manager with a guitar. As a bandleader, that workload multiplies. I'm usually the one lining up the gigs, which means I'm responsible for everything that follows. Allow me to enlighten you on the glamorous life of running a band. (Spoiler alert: it doesn't include Grammy Awards, but it *does* include Google Sheets.)

My days are filled with booking the gigs themselves (a chore that's like being stuck in an eternal loop of "We'll get back to you soon"—except they never do). I also need to hire musicians to play said gigs, write up contracts and invoices, liaise with venues about logistics, send quotes to potential clients, post on social media, fill out W-9s, learn song requests, prepare sheet music for the band, answer client emails with the subject line "Quick Question," and, best of all, purchase insurance.

Yes, *insurance*! It's absurd that I've had to become versed in liability insurance. I don't remember them offering an "Advanced Insurance for Jazz Guitarists" course at music school.

And, if I've booked a wedding, there's even *more* logistics to grapple with: timelines, first dances, introductions, toasts, "must-plays," and "absolute-do-not-plays." There are also always texts from the bride, like "My cousin Bobby plays guitar. Can he play three songs with you guys?" It takes an enormous amount of preparation to make it all look effortless—though it's hard to feel rock-and-roll when you're constantly editing a document called "Song Requests FINAL.doc."

Good thing I'm organized, or else the drummer's cousin would be singing, the bassist would be in the wrong venue, and the saxophonist would be juggling tambourines while the bride cries.

The Most Critical Details: Food and Clothes

All that planning eventually leads to two critical questions: What are we wearing, and will we be fed?

It's my job to confirm some crucial details in advance, and one of the most important of those is band attire, since every gig has its own unique "look." For clubs or other public events, we pretty much wear whatever makes us feel both cool and comfortable. But private events are a whole different matter. We're basically mannequins at the client's mercy. They might request anything from Hawaiian shirts to tuxedos—or, more recently, Great Gatsby attire for all the Prohibition-themed events that are all the rage these days.

Nothing shouts "roaring '20s" like sweating in a flat cap and wool vest in July. It feels more like roaring '90s!

But really, everything else is secondary to the most pressing question about any upcoming performance, one that's especially close to my heart (and stomach).

Two hours before every gig, I can always count on texts from my band members asking, "Hey, man. Do we get fed tonight?" It is helpful to know in advance, and it's greatly appreciated when we're taken care of, i.e., being granted permission to raid the buffet. I'm always a much happier musician when I have some nourishment in my belly.

I've dined like royalty and eaten in restaurants I would've been asked to leave if I weren't playing there. But it's not always like that. Sometimes, while guests are enjoying surf and turf, we're stuck with "bandwiches," crappy little sandwiches that scream, "You're hired help." Nothing fuels me for a dance set quite like peanut butter and cheese bandwiches. Oh, and we must make sure to eat them in the back room. God forbid guests see the barbaric vulgarity of musicians *eating*.

The most extreme example came from a super-rich country club in Connecticut, where I used to play. The guests ate from a massive buffet with lobster, filet mignon, and other French dishes I couldn't pronounce. Their plates would be overflowing with food, but they wouldn't even offer us a single, doggone breadstick! It's particularly upsetting when you know that, afterward, the leftovers went into the garbage. Yup, the raccoons ate better than we did. I sat in my car with a crummy bagged lunch.

One of the more absurd sights is the post-gig scramble after a cocktail hour. As our last note fades, we make a mad dash to the food trays to nab any leftover scraps before the wait staff whisks them away. I'm stuffing my face with stale cheese cubes, crackers, and grapes while plates are disappearing around me. Playing gigs has unquestionably helped me master the art of shoveling food. I've turned into Kobayashi at Nathan's Famous Hot Dog Eating Contest, and I could probably slam a plate of stuffed mushrooms in thirty seconds flat.

On most gigs, we typically eat during a set break. However, Murphy's Law dictates that our food will arrive precisely two minutes before we're due back onstage—every time! This has only contributed to my bad habit of eating too fast, one I've unfortunately brought home with me, much to my family's disgust. I'm trying to be more mindful these days, to slow down and actually *taste* my food.

Zen and the Art of Being a Sideman

Being a bandleader means that you're the boss, travel agent, and complaint department all rolled into one. Sometimes it's just a lot easier to be a sideman and let someone else deal with all of the emails that begin, "Hey, just a reminder that it's a surprise party. Can your band set up two hours early?" I appreciate the times when all I have to do is show up, play guitar, and leave without having to wait around to get paid and pack up the P.A.

But leading my own bands for so many years has also made me a much better sideman. When it's *not* my gig, I show up drama-free, happy to be there, with no complaints about money, tunes, or drummers (well, maybe the drummer).

If I've taken the job, I've accepted the terms, so it's unfair to whine about it. I've been on the other side way too often and know what a drag it is to listen to your bass player moan about not getting as big a fan as the singer did.

I'm happy to offer help to whomever *is* running the band if they want it. If they need a hand loading in the P.A., I'm available. If they want help picking songs, I'll offer ideas but happily play whatever they decide, even if I know it'll clear the dance floor. I'll even smile and say, "Yeah, man, it's totally in A," even though we all know it's in B flat. It's sure nice to relinquish the reins sometimes.

Oh Yeah, the "Music"

By now, you might be wondering, "Geez, does this dude ever play guitar?" (Along with "Does this dude ever stop complaining?") It's a fair question. Let's finally get to talking about music and the preparation it requires.

People don't realize how much practice is involved in simply becoming competent at one's instrument, let alone staying that way. I've admittedly always been a bit more zealous than most. In college, I'd practice for six hours a day, on average. I'd *run* back from class and immediately start woodshedding. Somewhere in there, I'd inhale a bowl of pasta before getting right back to it. While my practice time has lessened over the years and I'm not nearly as neurotic about it as I was then, I still practice most days for a couple of hours, unless I have a gig that day. It's just part of my daily routine at this point and has become a kind of sanctuary. I was always haunted by an expression used to terrorize us at school: "If you don't practice, someone else will." I still live under that fear, and I wish that "someone else" would take a nap every once in a while.

Of course, the learning never ends. Even after music school, I continued taking lessons from some of the most outstanding musicians around. Besides sitting at the feet of several prominent jazz guitarists, I took a correspondence course with the legendary pianist and teacher Charlie Banacos, who was from Boston. His material was intense and transformative, and I could spend a lifetime trying to master it all. There is always something to learn, and you'll never reach the top of the mountain if you want to keep improving. There will always be a new concept to work on, a new playing technique, a solo to transcribe, or a new tune to learn. Even to this day, when I feel stagnant, I push myself to seek out new resources and new ideas, which YouTube has made readily available.

I'm often asked, "What else is there to know at this point?" to which I laugh. Clearly, these folks don't play jazz for a living.

While it may sound conceited, people often say, "Wow, you're so talented." Maybe what they *really* mean is neurotic, overworking, and obsessive. While I appreciate the kind words, I'm quick to point out that I actually had to work awfully hard at this. By no means did I just wake up one day with Van Halen's "Eruption" at my fingertips. I've spent so much time working on music that my guitars have probably considered filing restraining orders against me.

I've heard it said that "an amateur musician will practice something until they get it right, but a professional will practice it until they can't get it wrong." I've come to appreciate the wisdom in these words more each day.

Yes, I practice a lot. But what about rehearsing with a band? You might imagine we get together all of the time to practice and "jam." Nope. Here's a secret: Many professional bands don't rehearse at all. We only do it when *absolutely* necessary, like learning a ton of original music or prepping a stage show with lots of production—and thankfully, those run-throughs are usually paid.

I'm fortunate to play with musicians at a level where rehearsals are rarely required. Sure, we'll get song requests we'll need to learn, or we pick new songs to add to our repertoire—but it's assumed everyone will do their homework and come prepared to play them cold. Admittedly, part of this is laziness. Mostly, everyone is too busy to find an agreeable time, but we're all pros who shouldn't need to get together to learn "Wonderwall."

Most of the time, this works out fine. The others? Well…that's when things get "musically adventurous." I'm apologizing now to any couple whose first dance we butchered. Live music means anything can happen and no amount of rehearsal keeps things from going sideways *sometimes*.

But through botched arrangements, ear-piercing feedback, and failing equipment, experience has taught me another valuable lesson in this job: the art of remaining stoic while everything around you falls apart—that's right, smile and carry on as if everything is unfolding exactly as planned. And trust me, I've smiled through some spectacular meltdowns, like a flight attendant cheerfully serving drinks while the wing is engulfed in flames. If you sell it well enough, most of the audience just assumes it's part of the show.

One of my worst all-time train wrecks happened when I was hired to put a Beach Boys tribute band together for a New Year's Eve event in Cape Cod. We went in cold—no rehearsal—and it was the first time I had even met the singer/keyboard player in person. Everything was going smoothly, until we got to "California Girls." It started well enough with the iconic organ intro, just like the record. But as soon as everyone came in together, it sounded like we'd dropped our instruments down a flight of stairs.

We all looked at each other like we were trying to figure out who killed Colonel Mustard with the lead pipe—then realized we were all playing in different keys. (In hindsight, that was probably something we should have discussed. Oops.) We had to stop mid-song, figure out the key, and negotiate a new one—all in front of an audience of about 500 amused onlookers. I wanted to crawl into the back of my amp and disappear. And yet, there I was, that flight attendant topping off champagne glasses with fake perkiness while the plane plummeted straight into the ground.

But that kind of situation is always looming more than you'd imagine. In professional settings, it's common to end up on a gig with musicians you don't know and no rehearsal. Sometimes we meet each other... onstage... and it's a bit of a musical trust fall, although nobody is quite sure who is catching whom.

Non-musicians often wonder how we can simply get together and play with people we've never met before, but at a certain level it's expected that we already know the repertoire of songs we're being called to play. It's essential to show up prepared; sometimes you only get one shot to get it right.

How About Making Something Original?

Note that none of this—the cheese cubes at the buffet, the insurance, the '20s garb—has anything to do with being creative or making art. They're simply the nuts and bolts of keeping the train on the tracks.

All the duties I've outlined make up the bare minimum for simply showing up and playing what's expected, when it's expected, and how it's expected. But I've always aspired to go beyond being just another working musician. I wanted to be an *artist* (not all musicians are artists) and develop a unique voice. Famous artists have a team to handle most of these chores, leaving them free to create.

For the rest of us, finding time for imagination is almost a miracle when there is so much daily work to do. But when the spark ignites and inspiration strikes, a new tune flows out, and for a few glorious minutes, you remember exactly why you deal with all this chaos…even if you'll have to document it with an invoice.

Let me tell you more about making something original.

6

You Can Go Your Own Way

Over the years, I played with artists in just about every style imaginable—rock, pop, reggae, jazz—and in just about every situation imaginable: cover bands, pit orchestras, tribute acts, and whatever else needed a guitarist with a vehicle. Have guitar, will travel—and travel I did, with anyone who called.

None of these performers ever lit up the Billboard charts, but I enjoyed playing with most of them, or at least learned something useful along the way. For instance, when a singer says, "Follow me," what they really mean is, "Good luck—you're on your own."

And when they have a bad night, it's usually because of "monitor issues."

That early education taught me two things: how to adapt quickly, and how to keep moving. I didn't know it yet, but that combination would become the defining skill of my entire career.

While I was building a reputation as a freelance guitarist, I also started forming my own bands and writing original music. In college, I formed a contemporary jazz (or "fusion") band blending jazz with rock, funk, and Latin influences. I was diving deeper into jazz but still had one foot firmly planted in the rock world. As a result, the music ended up somewhere between Jimi Hendrix and Miles Davis.

My first band was called "That's That," and some of the first gigs I ever played were with this band. We performed a few original tunes along with some jazz covers at a little club in West Orange, New Jersey, called Wallace's.

Sadly, it no longer exists. It was adjoined to a liquor store, which conveniently supplied both our courage and our audience.

We would play to about 10 people, clearing only $20 each. Yet it was a thrill to play music I had written to a group of people who technically qualified as a "crowd" under most fire codes. Gigs were few and far between, so every one felt like we were playing Coachella—if Coachella served pretzels and had a two-drink minimum.

And the Crowd Goes Mild

By 1997, I had written enough material to fill an album, so I decided to record and release one myself. I was already a composer, booking agent, and manager—why not also be a producer, record label, and financier? (The catch: Explaining to my accountant that my ROI depended on people not asking "Where's your singer?" wasn't a conversation I looked forward to.)

I recruited my regular band at the time—James Rosocha on bass and Brendan Buckley on drums. I also brought in a few new guys, including a killer saxophone player I discovered by accident while wandering through Greenwich Village one night. He was tearing it up with a blues band and completely knocked me out. I introduced myself and asked him if he'd play on my album. That's how Geoff Mattoon became a part of my world, and he still plays with me to this day.

With the addition of a few other players to round out the band, I was set to make my masterpiece. I booked time at a friend's home studio and began work. Admittedly, I had minimal studio experience and no idea how to produce a record, plus my writing was still a poor imitation of my heroes—not a recipe for success.

Needless to say, when the album was finished, I was disappointed with the results. My writing and playing had developed so much, even during the time it took to make that recording, that I knew I could do better. Still, I released "Tell the World" later that year and tried to believe that "artistic fulfillment" would outrun my credit card statements.

It was a start, and I was determined to keep moving forward. I would sell CDs to friends and at gigs, and even got reviews in a few jazz magazines. I was already getting better at booking gigs. What I lacked in business education, I made up for in persistence. I cold-called venues, mailed out demo tapes, and booked gigs anywhere that would have me—restaurants, cafés, bookstores, any structure with an outlet and a corner to set up.

I was persuasive enough that even I was beginning to believe my own emails. I'd take anything. I would only later become more strategic by googling the venue *before* accepting a gig.

One of my first steady jazz gigs was the now-defunct Borders bookstore chain, which used to have live music on weekends. I'd make $50 plus a $25 gift certificate to the store, and I accumulated so many of them that I could finally buy the CDs I had already pirated. Along with a drummer friend, I even booked my first tour through the Northeast and Midwest, playing almost entirely in bookstores. It was over a week and stretched from New Jersey to Wisconsin.

Let me tell you, it takes a special type of focus to practice the art of making jazz while trying not to notice someone flipping through cookbooks. Interestingly, I always found the best acoustics to be somewhere between the romance and self-help sections.

By 1999, I was ready to record again. I had a whole new batch of tunes ready to go, and had learned so much from the mistakes I'd made the first time around that I was determined to do better. My

And the Crowd Goes Mild

sophomore release, "Lost and Found," was a big step forward—better writing, better playing, better production—and this time, I felt genuinely proud of what I'd made, as measured by the number of times I *didn't* need to drop the word "jazz" to explain away my mistakes.

I even added "marketing department" to my list of duties by hosting and promoting my first-ever CD release party in Trenton, NJ, later that year.

Up to that point, everything I'd done had been powered by pure will and stubbornness. If something happened, it was because I made it happen—by booking it, paying for it, plugging it, or believing in it harder than anyone else had time to. I wasn't expecting a breakthrough so much as I was hoping not to stall out.

So when someone finally showed up who didn't need convincing—who heard the music and immediately said *yes*—it felt less like luck and more like validation. Like maybe all that pushing uphill had finally reached a flatter stretch of road.

Fast-forward to 2003. I was nearly finished working on my third album, "Simple Life," when a guy named Steve (I'll just use his first name) called me up out of the blue. He ran one of the first online music stores and really liked my stuff. He wanted to arrange a recording session with other musicians of his choosing. He was vague, but I was intrigued and said, "Sure. Why not?"

Steve booked time at a high-end studio on Long Island called Cove City Sound Studios. It was exciting to work at such a venerable and storied place—you know, the kind with gold records on the wall and Grammys on the shelf. I even bumped into R&B singer Ashanti, who was finishing up a session while I was there.

For my session, Steve brought in the legendary jazz trumpeter Randy Brecker along with Billy Joel's original sax player, Richie Cannata (who also owned the studio). We re-recorded a couple of my songs with these luminaries playing on them. To this day, I'm not sure what he intended to do with it, and nothing ever came from it, but still, I got to be in a great studio listening to two musical giants play on some songs of mine. It was a bit surreal.

Not long after, Steve launched his own jazz label and signed me as one of its first artists. As I was nearly finished with my third album, we agreed I would finish it as planned, and his new venture, Apria Records, would release it. Now, when I say "release" it, I mean that loosely, as Apria had no distribution or promotion yet, and the only thing that made my album part of the label was having their logo slapped onto the artwork. Once the album was finished, I promoted it myself with a CD release party in Princeton, NJ, because nothing says "global launch" like central New Jersey.

But the next time around, Steve offered to fund the whole thing, release it, and promote it as any traditional record company would. For the first time, I wasn't paying studio bills myself. That freedom was intoxicating—and dangerous.

And the Crowd Goes Mild

The album "Tomorrow's Too Late" became my most ambitious project yet. I felt I'd been given the chance to follow my imagination and make my own Sgt. Pepper. I wrote dense arrangements, hired a small army of incredible musicians, and treated the studio like a playground. For the first time, I wasn't counting studio hours or doing mental math every time someone suggested an overdub. I told myself this was how real records were made—without hesitation, without compromise, without constantly glancing at the meter running.

I didn't go full Axl Rose and hire a personal guru, but I definitely tested the limits of what "creative freedom" looks like when someone else is footing the bill. Admittedly, I became a bit overzealous—like a sheltered child who got his first taste of freedom at college (minus the throw-up). Although I was exhausted by the end of it, the results were the best I'd ever achieved. I was immensely proud of it—even if I suspected my mom might be the only one who would buy a copy.

I made two more records for Apria Records, "Straight Up" in 2007 and "Hit It and Quit" in 2009. "Straight Up" was a bit of a backlash to my previous release. I loved how "Tomorrow's Too Late" came out, but I wanted to make something much simpler this time. So, I wrote some scaled-down, jammier songs and brought a quartet to record them live in the studio—Joe Ashlar on keys, James Rosocha on bass, and Tom Cottone on drums.

Taking a live band into the studio was new territory for me. I could never have afforded a studio big enough to make this before I was part of this label.

To this day, it remains my personal favorite: funky, raw, organic, and infused with the live energy a jazz album should have. I even like most of my playing on it, which suggests either maturity or hearing loss.

JazzImprov magazine even said this about the recording: "Straight Up is so there, so ideal, so darn near perfect that it makes a listener want to head straight up there in a pilgrimage to quality-quality of musicianship, quality of recording, quality of what we all seek but seldom truly achieve." I usually don't care about reviews, unless they tell me how great I am.

I had written and recorded so much music in the previous couple of years that my notebooks were nearly empty. However, not long after I released "Straight Up," Steve was already asking me to write music for another album he wanted to make with a great drummer named Joel Rosenblatt. Joel was a member of the well-known contemporary jazz group Spyro Gyra for many years, but had recently left the band and was now looking for other projects.

Writing for someone else was a new challenge that I was very excited about, so I got right to work. I began composing music that drummers would find interesting—rhythmic, a variety of grooves, and plenty of odd time signatures. But in the end, Joel decided that it would be better to make it *my* album, and he'd just play on it. That was fine by me. I was going to ride this train as long as it was on the tracks, so I was happy to get right back to work. That album would become "Hit It and Quit."

To record it, we once again returned to Cove City Sound Studios and I was able to hire an all-star band

And the Crowd Goes Mild

to record it: Joel Rosenblatt on drums, Will Lee on bass (he most famously played in David Letterman's Late Show band as well as on thousands of albums and jingles), and Nick Rolfe (Aretha Franklin, Sting, Bruce Springsteen) on piano. I recruited my longtime saxophone buddy, Geoff Mattoon.

The album sounded amazing, and I was grateful to have been given the opportunity to make it. I even had a CD release party for it with the same band at the legendary club, Iridium, near Times Square, NYC. Playing a live gig with those titans at that prestigious venue was one of my most cherished musical accomplishments, and still is. I was on a high.

And then, just as suddenly, it was over.

At the time, signing with Apria felt like a turning point. For the first time, someone else believed in my music enough to underwrite it—studio time, musicians, artwork—the things I'd always paid for myself. I allowed myself to imagine that this was what came next: a label that would handle the release, the promotion, even the parts of the business I'd been trying to do myself for years. It felt like all the hard work had finally paid off. The machine might finally be working without me pushing it uphill.

Steve was my biggest cheerleader, always talking about new music, worldwide distribution, and how things were "about to break." I wanted to believe him, and mostly I did. But emails grew vaguer, timelines slipped, and releases quietly stalled, and I chalked it up to growing pains. Jazz, after all, has never been known for moving quickly.

Around this time, Steve started going off the rails. He was from Missouri, and we'd always meet up whenever he was in New York. His company was growing fast, and he always had a recording session going on, but I could tell he was partying a little too much, and he looked worse every time I saw him. I also began hearing similar stories from other musicians—bills weren't being paid, people couldn't reach him, and nothing ever seemed to move forward.

Then, without ceremony, Steve disappeared. Just vanished. Calls went unanswered. Emails bounced into the void. The label simply stopped existing, and I never heard from him again. I was grateful for the experience—the studios, the musicians, the albums I never could have afforded otherwise—but the ending still stung. There was no explosion, no dramatic phone call, no final argument. The whole thing simply dissolved. One day, I was part of a label, and the next day it was as if it had never existed.

I told myself I was lucky—and I was. I'd made records I never could have afforded and played with musicians I'd admired for years. Still, it felt like being quietly uninvited from a party I thought I belonged at. When the noise faded, I was left with the same question I'd always had: "Now what?" I was back where I started—making records by myself again. Cheap ones.

I released a live album in 2010 titled "Five and Live," named for the quintet I had on those live gigs, and followed it up with a traditional jazz album titled "Ready or Not." While I never felt like a truly traditional or "straight-ahead" jazz guitarist, I love playing that music. Both of these recordings were a departure for me and could be made on my own.

In 2015, while on tour in the UK, someone offered to record one of our gigs for *free*. How could I turn that down? In all honesty, the audio fidelity was a mere step above voicemail from 1996. But hey, you get what you pay for, and I had never documented my touring trio—live and raw. I released it under the oh-so-creative title "Live in the UK!" and naturally, people overseas really liked it.

After those live albums—which are the convenient equivalent of, "This should hold them for a while"—I was itching to make a big contemporary studio record again. It had been several years, and I'd accumulated lots of new material. But the issue became how to pay for it. Even though I'd recently set up a small studio in my basement and could do some of the work from home, I knew the album I wanted to make would be expensive.

So, in 2016, I ran a Kickstarter campaign and successfully crowdfunded the project, which became the album "Manifesto." I got very creative with my giveaways—half of one of my guitar solos seems to belong to a guy in Minnesota.

The album turned out great, and I was really proud of it. I named it "Manifesto" because it's a statement about what I love in music as well as a representation of my musical values. It's dense, complex, interesting, and highly produced with lots of orchestration and development. I adore thoughtful music with strong attention to writing.

Just to keep everyone on their toes, I made a wild left turn for the next album as I became interested in making electronic music. I'd been experimenting with it for a while, but never knew exactly what to do with the music I made. These pieces weren't repetitive beats over one chord; they were *songs*. I made fully realized compositions and applied the same love of writing that I'd always put into my jazz music.

I started with four pieces and submitted them to a few music libraries, hoping they might be placed in TV shows (more on this later). To my delight, a couple were actually picked up. One ended up on the MTV show *Catfish*, and another appeared in a few episodes of *The Real Housewives of Atlanta* on Bravo. I always knew my music was perfect for dating, deception, and angry, drunken dinner parties.

This only encouraged me to write more. The songs were free to make; I could work on them at my leisure and hopefully make a little money off them. So I set out to write six more, filling an entire album. I changed the styles and beats to encompass genres such as techno, ambient, game music, EDM, house, and more.

When I finished all ten, I sent them off to try to get them placed, then released the whole collection for downloads and streaming under the title "Electronic Etudes." I honestly didn't expect other people to like it very much (if they listened at all), but it was music I had worked hard on, and I wanted it out in the universe.

I kept making records because that's what I knew how to do. Different formats, different styles,

And the Crowd Goes Mild

different budgets—but always forward motion. On paper, it looked productive. From the outside, it looked healthy.

Inside, though, something was thinning out. I wasn't out of ideas—I was out of urgency. The question wasn't whether I *could* keep making music. It was whether there was any reason to keep releasing it into a world that barely noticed. Consequently, I wasn't writing much anymore, wasn't feeling inspired, and didn't see the point in releasing anything new. It would take something drastic to change my mind.

Well, that "something drastic" happened, and life changed for *everyone*. I had been flirting with the idea of slowing down for a while, but I never quite allowed myself to stop. Then the decision was made for me.

When COVID hit, *everything* stopped. Not gradually—instantly. Gigs vanished, tours were canceled, calendars emptied, and the phone went silent. For the first time in decades, nobody needed me to be anywhere with a guitar.

I honestly welcomed the break. I'd been burned out for quite a while and hadn't quite admitted it to myself. I'd often thought about stepping off the treadmill for a bit, and suddenly I had no choice—and no guilt. Still, once the novelty wore off, something else crept in. If I wasn't gigging, wasn't recording, wasn't moving forward—what exactly was I?

Days blurred together. I watched the news like everyone else and tried not to think too far ahead. I had no idea when live music would come back, but that was ok. I was grateful for the rest. But an idea began germinating in my mind. I'd been playing solo instrumental guitar gigs for years and had always talked about making a solo guitar album, but I'd never quite found the time or the nerve. Now I had nothing but time, so I tentatively began working on it with no expectations. There was also no band to hide behind. No arrangements to distract from the playing. Just one guitar and a spirit of musical adventure.

I recorded "Sole Searching" alone in my home studio, slowly and carefully. Some days I worked for hours; other days I did nothing at all. It was uncomfortable and strangely calming at the same time. The album forced me to listen to myself in a way I hadn't before, and when it was finished, I realized something had shifted. It was a relief. Recording my solo guitar album also got my creative juices flowing again, and it made me realize I wasn't done yet. Not even close.

I began writing jazz tunes again and liked where they were heading. We were still in the middle of a global pandemic, and I had no idea whether I'd ever do anything with the music, but it felt good—so I sent it to a few musician friends to see what might come back. Since no one could go anywhere yet, everything had to be done remotely. I laid down the basic tracks and sent them out to some of my favorites to record in their home studios: Geoff Mattoon on sax, Dan Paul and Glenn McClelland on piano, Dave Edwards on bass, and Abe Fogle on drums.

This kind of recording has become strangely normal. You don't have to be in the same room, or even the same country, to make a record anymore. You send files, people add their parts, and everything comes

And the Crowd Goes Mild

back to be assembled later. I do plenty of sessions like this in my own home studio and often have no idea who else is on the production. It all lives in the cloud. That's how I made "It's Just a Dream," which I released in the fall of 2022, just as life was beginning to return to normal. It felt good—relieving, even—to be creative again.

Not knowing whether this was my last one, I wanted to go out with a bang. Two solos needed to be filled, so I asked Randy Brecker to play trumpet on one of them and guitarist Mike Stern, one of my long-time musical heroes, to play on the other. They're both absolute legends, but it was particularly meaningful to have one of my greatest influences and role models play on a song I had written.

I discovered Mike's music while I was in school, and after moving back home, I saw him regularly at a steady gig at the 55 Bar in New York's West Village, which was a total dive, and I mean that in the most endearing way possible. He always blew me away with his virtuosic blend of jazz, rock, and blues, and I was just as inspired by his writing as his playing. He was one of my most formative musical heroes, and I eventually got the courage to ask him if I could take some lessons with him. I would go to his apartment, sit in a room with him, and jam for an hour or so. He was always so gracious, humble, and encouraging, but I was still terribly nervous about asking him to play on my record.

Luckily, it went as well as I had rehearsed in the mirror several times—and he said yes.

Mike played on a tune called "Our Darker Angels," and his performance was beautiful. He even sang a harmony part, which added an unexpected depth to the track. Having Mike Stern on an album of mine was one of the most satisfying moments of my career—another long-held item crossed off the bucket list.

But I wasn't finished releasing music *just* yet. After a conversation with some music business types about the new distribution models and how music is released nowadays, I decided to try releasing a single. That's what the "kids are doing," and I thought it would be fun to release something without the pressure of having to make a whole album and the expense of printing up CDs. I had recently written a fun little jam called "Pop Tart," and at the end of 2024, dipped my toe into the modern world of singles by releasing that ditty into the streaming world.

Looking back, I realize the common thread wasn't success or failure—it was movement. Sometimes forward, sometimes sideways, sometimes in circles. I had so much creative energy and ambition that remaining still always felt like surrender. The world might have barely noticed my output, but it mattered to *me*. As an artist, I had something to say, and the need to say it always carried a sense of urgency. Making music has felt like releasing a pressure valve—it brought me some peace. And yet, there's still much more inside of me.

Is that finally the end of my recording career? Probably. Maybe. I don't know. Currently, I have no plans to write or release any more jazz records. But I've said that before…

7

Leaving On a Jet Plane

No musician's book would be complete without stories from the road. Yes—most musical memoirs are filled with lurid stories about groupies, drug overdoses, and general mayhem. But as I've said, this is a different kind of book. I'm going to describe what it's like being on the road for a small-time band rather than big-time rock stars, which can be even more absurd, particularly for my own tours, which have always been low-budget affairs.

There are no first-class hotels, limousines, or bottles of Cristal waiting in our green rooms. Instead, we get budget hotels, a station wagon, and too much time on our hands. I call it "guerrilla touring"; others have described it as a bunch of people driving around, smelling each other's farts. Honestly? That sounds about right.

I should point out that I've never had the assistance of a manager, booking agent, publicist, road crew, or any other professional. All those duties fall squarely on me; if I want to tour, I have to handle everything myself.

Early on, I would take my jazz trio on weekend jaunts around the Northeastern U.S.—Pennsylvania, New York State, maybe Vermont if we were feeling particularly adventurous. It was fun. We'd pack into my minivan, hit the road, and pretend we were on tour, escaping real life and the usual local gigs for a few days.

But things took an exciting turn in the early 2000s when my wife and I visited my uncle, who was living in London. For the heck of it, I took some demos (CDs in those days) of my band around town to see if anyone would be interested in booking us. I had zero expectations, but it was worth a shot since I didn't get to London very often.

Lo and behold, I found a club that offered us a week's worth of gigs. I was excited. The place was a total dive, sure. But it was in the heart of SoHo, and semi-famous because Amy Winehouse used to perform there before she was *Amy Winehouse*. Otherwise, it had little else going for it.

The pay? Not good.
The lodging? Couches in my uncle's cramped flat.
The adventure? Priceless.

And the Crowd Goes Mild

Besides, you don't get anywhere by playing it safe all the time, and thankfully, my band felt the same way.

Our overseas week was fantastic, despite the club's gear being so "vintage" it barely worked. And the crowds...well...the turnouts were somewhere between "intimate" and "imaginary." But it was *London*! After we finished performing each night, we'd go out and explore the SoHo nightlife.

On one occasion, we thought it would be fun to ride on top of a double-decker bus as it drove its entire route throughout the city. It was a beautiful night, and we enjoyed the scenic ride until it stopped at the outer edge of London at 2am for the driver's scheduled hour-long break. It was a long journey back into the city, and I don't think I got into bed until 5am.

We had such a great time that we returned the following year during our spring break from school (we were all teachers), but that time we also booked a few venues outside the city. Adding these gigs introduced a whole new set of problems to solve, including the need to rent a car, secure gear, and find places to stay, all of which were made easier by the internet and allowed us to travel to some new places, including a jazz festival in Wales.

That trip was a mixture of excitement, fun, terror, exhaustion, and stress. We had to navigate the country without a GPS, drive on the opposite side of the road, gather equipment for every gig, and find accommodations on a shoestring budget. Those early tours were austere. We crashed on people's couches and more than a few floors. And besides sharing the stage, we'd often have to share hotel beds to save money—and we *still* lost money, while also being a fire hazard.

But the gigs were worth it, and we knew these short outings could blossom into something epic. There was still so much to figure out, and we learned a great deal about making touring viable in a foreign country as we built up a solid following. But most impressively, I was now an *international artist*!

Our UK trip ultimately evolved into an annual adventure. I'd bring my trio back every Easter-time, taking any gig we could get, short of funerals—and even that was negotiable. If there were a power outlet and at least three walls, we'd call it a venue. And it all paid off. As people got to know us, the gigs got better, the crowds grew larger, and I eventually shifted our annual journey to summertime, when, as teachers, we had more time to be away.

It's always been the same trio, with James Rosocha on bass and Joe Falcey on drums, and we always sit in the same seats in the car: Joe drives, I sit in the front passenger seat (I am the tour manager, after all), and James sits in the back, protecting himself from gear falling on him. Year after year, we pack into a station wagon, drive thousands of miles, and play a whirlwind of gigs, winning over audiences, making new friends, and perfecting the art of living like homeless people.

Over the years, it's evolved into a real odyssey. In the summer of 2024, our tour was five weeks long with thirty-one gigs that included stops in the UK,

Belgium, the Netherlands, Germany, Luxembourg, and even our first date in Northern Ireland. Plus, I now return to the UK on my own a couple of times a year to play with some of the great local UK musicians I've met along the way. It's amazing how that one little weekend in London turned into an entire overseas career for me.

By now, I've toured the UK dozens of times and feel right at home, except for the ribbing I still suffer for my American accent. After years of being teased for pronouncing city names incorrectly (for example, Towcester is pronounced like "toaster" and Birmingham is "BER-ming-um," not "Ber-ming-HAM"), I feel I finally have a good handle on their accent and unique expressions, and can understand even the most slangy of conversations. "Blimey, mate, I was absolutely knackered after that dodgy curry, so I popped down the chippy, had a cheeky pint, watched footy on the tele, and now I'm mucking about with a cuppa until half five." I know what all that means!

I've also developed a love for tea, crumpets, and coronation chicken—and I'm a solid left-side-of-the-road driver.

Admittedly, it's a ton of work. I have to start arranging the tour about nine months in advance, as it's a complex puzzle with many moving parts. Besides booking the gigs and ensuring we have lodging every night, I also need to plan sensible routing to minimize driving, though sometimes it's impossible to avoid a long haul here and there.

People often criticize me for the zigzagging, seemingly random path the tour takes. But it's actually quite challenging to arrange it in any semblance of a logical order. There are times we'll have to drive to a city a few hours away, only to come back a day or two later. This inevitably leads to a question that *really* annoys me: "Why can't you book your gigs in a nice straight path?"

Oh, you innocent little lamb. I wish it were that simple. Do you think I've *never* considered that? Do you think I just *love* the hours and hours of extra "us" time in the car? The simplest answer is that venues have their own schedules too. And besides, we don't want to play in one place too often. An appearance in a particular town should be an *event*—we don't want people saying, "Eh, I'll catch them next week." And once those decisions are made, you're left to live with the consequences.

But making the schedule is only part of the story—*living* it is where the real fun begins. Let me show you what that actually looks like.

After thousands of miles, you learn quickly that being "on the road" is basically being homeless with an itinerary. You come to know highway rest stops intimately—often saying things like "Oh, this is the one with the KFC back by the bathroom." Long hours in the car get dull, and after a couple of days, we've exhausted nearly every topic of conversation. So we find ways to keep ourselves occupied and our minds sharp—memorizing trivia like U.S. capitals, U.S. presidents, European capitals, and, most recently, the NATO phonetic alphabet (Alpha,

Bravo, Charlie, etc.). I'll admit it, we're really just a bunch of... November, Echo, Romeo, Deltas.

We also bring trivia books, joke books, and podcasts or audiobooks to listen to. More often than not, though, we're just sitting there with nothing to do but, yup, smell each other's farts.

Tour life alternates between boredom and chaos. There are stretches where you have nowhere to be and nothing to do. For instance, you might have to check out of your hotel room by 10am but not be at that night's gig until 8pm. If it's only an hour away, that leaves hours to burn. Sometimes we play tourist and visit local sights, but there isn't always something exciting to see—or maybe there is, and we've already seen it. On rare occasions, all we can think to do is find a nearby park and lie in the grass, imagining what people with "real jobs" are doing while we argue if that cloud is a giraffe or a cat with a top hat.

Other days are the complete opposite. We'll drive all day or spend hours dealing with logistical chores—replacing a piece of gear, fixing something on the car—and arrive at the venue already worn out. More often than not, I don't even get a chance to touch my instrument until showtime, which isn't ideal. The music we play is demanding, and its improvisational nature requires imagination and a constant search for new musical ground. Showing up stressed, tired, and cold is the last thing I want. I'm at my best when we can check into a hotel early, grab a nap, and squeeze in a shower before showtime.

But if you look at my social media, you might think we just appear in beautiful places, play fantastic venues for wonderful audiences, and gallivant around like Peter Pan. I'm just as complicit in selling this dream because I'm not showing everyone the other twenty hours of the day—the long, exhausting, sometimes ridiculous hours spent just getting from gig to gig. Some drives are grueling due to the distance, traffic, or both.

In major European cities, we're constantly battling congestion, bicyclists, one-way streets, and throngs of pedestrians to reach a venue. And when road signs are unfamiliar, everything becomes more confusing. On more than a few occasions, we've mistakenly driven down pedestrian-only streets, dodging angry onlookers cursing us out in some foreign language accentuated with colorful hand gestures. We've spent way too much time navigating a labyrinth of one-way streets, searching for parking, and trying to decipher parking meters in a language we don't understand. Simple tasks become complicated, exhausting, and sometimes infuriating. And yet, hours later, we still need to perform, be "on," and make it look like none of those headaches ever happened.

We joke that after a full day of "go, go, go," we arrive at the venue washed out and hungry, unload the car, set up, and the night has only just begun. Now it's *time to be creative*! Yes, spend all day putting out fires and then casually invent art in front of strangers.

And yet, we do it. All the stress, confusion, and exhaustion vanish the moment the music starts. That's why we're there—and when it's time to play, we're gonna *play*!

And the Crowd Goes Mild

At the *end* of the night, you might think there's a rowdy after-party to attend. Ha! Sure, there are always people who want to keep the good times going with us afterward, but there's no road crew to pack up the car. No manager to get paid. And there's still a crowd of people we need to say hello to. By that point, all the pubs are likely closed, so it's back to the hotel with a bed and some decent Wi-Fi. *That's* when the drugs come out...Advil. Taken responsibly.

When we were younger, we went out a lot, but we learned that it's a rookie move. It's simply not possible to function after going so many nights without sleep, yet having so much traveling to do. Your health will suffer, as will the music, and for us, the music always comes before anything else.

And yet, we're always tired—it just becomes a way of life. The combination of late nights, a different bed every night, and always being on the move isn't a good recipe for restful sleep. Add to that a room full of snoring that sounds like dueling chainsaws—thank the tour gods for earplugs.

I often fantasize about having a driver to chauffeur us, a crew to manage our gear, and a bus to sleep on. Those spoiled rock stars don't know how good they have it!

This kind of travel also takes a toll on your diet, because it's so easy to eat poorly. Roadside rest stops are convenient but expensive, so we prefer grocery stores to find a better bargain and healthier grub. It takes some creativity to figure out where to stash all our food, and we've become masters of utilizing every crevice in the car.

The glove box? That's my pantry.
Seat pockets? Snack drawers.
Cup holders? Liquor cabinet.

At this point, our station wagon is part tour van, part mobile convenience store, and part hoarder's wet dream.

One of the worst scenarios that can happen is showing up for a gig that's been double-booked. You arrive at the venue, and another band is already set up, or vice versa. It's a super awkward situation. Someone has to go home, and whether that includes compensation is subject to negotiation.

This happened to us once many years ago while on tour in the UK. We showed up to a gig in Thornbury, England, just as another band was setting up. A mistake had been made—but it wasn't ours. In a particularly diplomatic gesture and an exercise in international cooperation, we all agreed that both bands would alternate sets and then jam together at the end. What began as a headache turned into a genuinely fantastic evening. We loved watching each other play and ended the night as friends. That other band was led by a phenomenal UK saxophonist/vocalist named Kim Cypher, and, since that encounter, we've stayed close and have collaborated on many gigs and recordings. To this day, we try to play together any time I'm in the UK. Oh, and crisis averted—we both got paid—although I still insist it was *our* gig.

Another ongoing challenge while on tour is simply not losing your stuff. Misplacing belongings is a recurring nightmare. I've left behind many more toothbrushes and phone chargers than I care to admit, along with clothes, musical gear, and once, even my entire suitcase! Because of that, I'm constantly checking and rechecking that everything is accounted for and in its designated place; otherwise, it's probably gone. Most musicians buy souvenirs in each city: I leave them.

I've also learned never to unpack my suitcase, or I'll have to pack it all again the next day. Nothing comes out of it that doesn't *need* to. Out of habit, I do the same thing on vacation now, even when I'm staying somewhere for a full week.

But staying anywhere isn't part of this job. We're always on the move. I try to book gigs nearly every night we're on the road, because traveling has the audacity to cost money. On earlier tours, we played *every* night—even doubles—because the pay was meager and our standards were negotiable. Yeah, we took *anything*

It's not always easy to book Mondays or Tuesdays, but we'd generally take any gig that paid a little, put some food in our bellies, and gave me a chance to sell a few CDs. I've lived by the expression "If you're not appearing, then you're disappearing." I'd much rather be out playing than sitting in a hotel room watching "The Bachelor."

Having toured for many years, the gigs have improved dramatically, and we can now afford to take a couple of days off to catch our breath. But while it's nice to rest a little, getting reacquainted with some couch time sometimes makes it even *harder* to get going again.

You might be wondering: *if it's all so dull, stressful, and arduous, why do you do it?* The answer is simple: we get to play the music we love, the way we want to play it, to crowds that want to hear it. We feel truly appreciated overseas, playing to folks who travel for miles, sometimes on multiple nights, to let us know that music matters. People show up, they pay attention, and they clap at the right moments. There have been times when we've moved audience members to tears, or they've come up to us after a gig to excitedly tell us that it was one of the best performances they'd ever seen. I find that hard to believe, and while I never let it get to my head, it's still awfully nice to hear. We've put so much work into honing our craft, and it's validating to play for music lovers who care and generously show their appreciation. And as much as I moan about the travel, it's a privilege to be able to visit places that I would never see otherwise, to share our art and get paid for it.

Along the way, we've built relationships with people we now see year after year under happy circumstances. They often put us up and we're truly grateful for their hospitality; without it, these tours probably wouldn't be viable. It's difficult to turn a profit with the expense of flights, cars, fuel, food, and earplugs in bulk.

With all that in mind, you're also probably wondering: *Are you making any money doing this, or is it just for the stories and the chips?* The short answer is, yes, we turn a modest profit. But I'd point out that I'd make a lot more if we just stayed home and played it safe with our usual local gigs. It's never been about money. Comfort doesn't invite adventure, and safety never made for good stories.

To any would-be road warriors out there, I'll offer a few pro tips of great importance that are often learned the hard way, so take note. First, always keep your rental car key on a carabiner, and make it a habit to secure it to something when you're not using it. There have been too many close calls when we thought we'd lost it, which would've made for a terrible day.

Next, buy booze at a duty-free shop whenever you come across one, and stash it in the car. It's so much cheaper, and you don't have to spend as much time and money seeking out a post-gig shot at pubs.

Third, always keep a few shopping bags with napkins and plastic utensils in the car for when you buy food at the grocery store. We pride ourselves on the bags we keep crumpled under our seats, and we're never upset about not having napkins handy while eating in the car.

Lastly, fill up your gas tank whenever you find cheap gas rather than waiting until the tank is almost empty and you're forced into the nearest option. In the long run, it keeps more money in your pocket. These are simple lessons from a larger toolkit we've acquired for life on the road.

So there it is, years of touring distilled into a few helpful nuggets.

With all of the improvisation on stage, there's just as much offstage. A flat tire in Belgium? Figure it out.

Broken amp in the Netherlands? Improvise. Customs official blocking the ferry? Smile, shrug, and mutter something vaguely apologetic. Problem-solving becomes a skill set you never knew you needed, because there are always mishaps!

Amazingly, even with all the setbacks, I'm proud to say we've never missed *one* gig. Not one! We've come close. Case in point: our infamous trip from the UK to Brugge, Belgium, via the Eurotunnel Train. Picture this: eight hours of gridlock at the English Channel crossing because French customs decided to be extra cranky after Brexit. We missed our train—and the next 10 after that. Technically, we didn't miss the gig—they rescheduled it—but eight hours in a traffic jam will definitely make you question your bladder's structural integrity.

Touring is a paid, chaotic, endlessly fascinating adventure that keeps us on our toes, tests our patience, builds camaraderie, and rewards us with unforgettable experiences. We learn to pack strategically, memorize useless facts, and navigate foreign streets while maintaining the delicate balance between being both musicians and hobos.

At the end of the day—or more accurately, the end of a five-week, 30-something gig whirlwind—we look back and realize that all the planning, the difficulties, and the logistical nightmares were worth it. We've performed, traveled, met incredible people, and survived on a mix of snacks, musical euphoria, and sheer lunacy. As the miles add up and the suitcases begin to smell like a gym locker room, every mistake, mishap, and unexpected adventure becomes part of the story. The stories—messy, funny, and completely unforgettable—are precisely why we keep doing it.

So let's get to those stories—the ones we can finally laugh about. Buckle up. The road is long, the station wagon is small, and the tales are endless. Welcome to guerrilla touring, my friends. And yes, the farts are included.

8

Highway to Hell

Every tour has a disaster. Not *might*. Not *sometimes*. Always.

Whenever my musical friends and I swap stories over drinks, we always say, "Man, I could write a book." Well, here it is. You can plan meticulously, pack efficiently, and leave early, but the road has a way of reminding you who's really in charge. Everything you're about to read is true—no exaggeration needed. Despite the setbacks, we've always found a way to reach the stage and give it everything we've got, like the road warriors that we are.

What follows is a collection of misadventures that made our lives miserable, tested our patience, and very nearly derailed entire tours. At the time, they were traumatic. Now they're considered "content."

Behold, *real* life on tour.

Standby Me

Some mishaps start with a flat tire, some with food poisoning; this one begins at Newark Airport in beautiful Newark, New Jersey.

It was an early summer's eve, and my trio showed up nice and early for a flight to London's Heathrow Airport, excited about another trip and the adventure that lay ahead. I had booked a 31-date tour, which included a day off at the beginning to collect our gear, get some rest, and reacclimate to our hobo lifestyle. While I was trying to make road life a little more tolerable for musicians now in their early fifties, the universe had other ideas.

When we got to the airport, the weather turned ugly. It was bad, like an audition for "The Perfect Storm"—torrential rain and hurricane-force winds. We were told our flight would be delayed by about an hour, which turned into another hour, which turned into a cancellation.

The United Airlines agent told everyone, "Go home and call the airline tomorrow." I was like, "Yeah, right." I worked too hard setting this all up just to turn around and give up that easily. I called the airline's customer service line right then and there, and she suggested we go to the top floor of the airport to speak with an airline employee in person.

And the Crowd Goes Mild

Unfortunately, everyone else had gotten the same advice. We stood in a line that stretched virtually the entire length of the terminal, a human snake of weariness and anger.

It was about midnight, and the line was crawling forward at a tortuously slow pace. Inch by inch, floor tile by floor tile, we crept closer to the desk. Our fatigue and grumpiness only exacerbated the tedium. At one point, we were sleeping on the filthy floor, rolling our bodies anytime the line crept even a little.

By 2am, all humor was gone. By 3am, hope had left with it. Finally, at about 4:30am, we reached the counter and spoke with an agent who could only tell us, dryly, "It looks like we can't get you on another flight for four days."

Four days? No! We couldn't wait four days. We'd start missing gigs, and we didn't miss gigs! I begged. I pleaded. I even considered bribery. She was unmoved and replied unsympathetically, "You could stay in the airport and wait on standby. Maybe something will open up sooner."

That suggestion offered a glimmer of hope, and we had to give it a shot. We'd tough it out at the airport for as long as it took. The United lounge opened at 5am, so we could at least get some good food and bad coffee before catching a little sleep. We claimed a few seats in the back corner, settled in, and tried to kill time before making another attempt that evening.

After a terribly boring day spent staring out the window, making futile efforts at some shut-eye, and feeling sorry for ourselves, we eventually walked back down to the United gates with a mix of anxiety and hope. The first flight out was completely full. The next flight left an hour later, with one seat available.

We held a brief band meeting, and it was agreed that I should take it. If the other guys couldn't get out that night, I could at least collect our car, gather our gear, and get a head start. We probably weren't going to be able to travel together anyway, so we were going to have to improvise.

An hour into my flight, I received a text from my drummer, Joe, letting me know he had gotten the last seat on the next flight out. A miracle. Another hour in, James got a spot on the next, and last, flight of the evening. My trio was airborne, albeit on three different airplanes. What a relief!

When I got to Heathrow, I picked up our rental car in the parking garage, reclined the seat, and proceeded to enjoy the deepest sleep of my life. I had barely slept for the previous 48 hours and was desperately tired. About an hour into my nap, I was awoken by a knock on the car window. I opened my eyes and, through a cloud of weary confusion, saw that it was Joe, who had just arrived. He joined me in the car, and I proceeded to take the second deepest nap of my life until James' arrival an hour later.

We were exhausted, foul-smelling, and haggard, but we'd made it. Unfortunately, our luggage hadn't. Apparently, our bags didn't share our spontaneity. Since we'd been on standby, our suitcases didn't travel with us, but there was no time to wait for them. We had to play our first gig *that* night, so we set off immediately. Our show "wardrobe" was the same disgusting clothing we'd worn for the last two days, as well as slept in, while on the floor of Newark Airport. We hoped for understanding audiences—and good ventilation.

We made it work. Was there any other choice? We traveled and performed, roughing it without suitcases or any personal effects until we were finally reunited with our luggage a week later. That's a whole week of smelling like we do at the *end* of a tour, although we hadn't actually earned it yet. After retrieving our things from Heathrow once again, I hugged my clean underwear and said, "I love you."

There seems to be one major disaster with every trip; this one just happened to be at the beginning. In retrospect, I was grateful for the extra travel day, but so much for using it to rest.

I'd also like to mention that this entire experience was documented in a YouTube series I created, chronicling our 2023 and 2024 tours.

Trio Interrupted

Like the rest of the world, COVID shut down our tours for a couple of years. While it was disappointing not to be able to travel during that time, it also provided a nice break and made us all the more excited to get back out there again.

Once the stages reopened, we were back out on the road. It was 2022, and only a few gigs into that trip, Joe started feeling a bit "off." We thought he'd perhaps eaten some questionable fish and chips. But what was "off" one night became full-blown sick the next. During a gig, he started feeling terrible, and he looked like a ghost. A rapid test confirmed it: COVID.

Typically, a sick bandmate is just an inconvenience. But consider the circumstances: a trio stuffed into one car, in constant proximity, and with a highly contagious ailment floating around. We couldn't leave him behind. He couldn't quarantine. What were we supposed to do? Our solution: Wear masks in the car and roll down the windows to let every gust of wind cleanse our lungs.

We drove to our next gig in Doveridge, England, where the promoter, bless him, found us a last-minute fill-in. We delivered Joe to a local hotel the way an Amazon driver drops off a package on your stoop, and went back to the venue to perform with our substitute drummer, Jon Broberg, and some "desperate improvisation." Jon is an excellent drummer, but the poor guy hardly knew anything we were playing. He did his best, though. It wasn't our most virtuosic showing, but it was a showing, nonetheless.

The next night, we were to play in London with legendary saxophonist and friend John Altman. Once again, we had to drop Joe off at an Airbnb and play the gig without him. It's hard to be a trio without a drummer, kind of like a three-legged chair. But we kept our balance; nobody got hurt, and we made it through yet another night.

The next several days were more of the same logistical headaches—driving with masks on, windows rolled down, and trying not to infect the innocent. All this while juggling hotel drop-offs and an itinerary of performances. Joe basically became another piece of luggage we'd pick up and drop off between gigs.

Just as he was getting healthy again and we thought we could finally relax and play a regular gig together, the unthinkable happened.

James caught COVID.

Touring: 2. Us: 0.

We were somewhere between a jazz trio and a mobile quarantine unit.

While these situations were troublesome and nerve-racking, they weren't scarring. So let me get to a few of those, since they're the experiences that both haunt and amuse me.

Touring: A Crash Course

Nothing like a sunny morning drive in the English countryside to remind you that life can have a dark sense of humor. We were driving up from Brighton, England, where we had played the night before, to an afternoon gig in Wolverhampton. It was just over a three-hour drive. Admittedly, we'd been up late the night before, having a bit of a "social outing." I wouldn't say we were "hungover" necessarily; let's call it "foggy."

It was early in our tour, and we had a double on this day. The sun was shining, and we enjoyed an uneventful journey north. Just as we were about to make the *final* turn into the venue—I mean, we could practically hear the applause—out of nowhere...*BAM*!! Another car came speeding around the corner like it was out of "Fast & Furious," and swiped the side of our car before spinning out into the grass. Joe's last-minute swerve prevented a devastating head-on crash, but it was enough to turn our car into a metal accordion.

As we staggered out of the car, trying to make sense of what had just happened, I had so many questions. *Do I still have my limbs? More importantly, is my guitar ok? How do we get another car? Will I have to pay for this one? Is the tour over? Have I died? I really thought heaven would have more food.*

We surveyed the damage and found the car to be completely smashed. He hit us hard, and we were lucky that everyone was alright—no injuries, no bruises, only shattered nerves. We'd had minor fender benders before but never a full-on accident, in a rental car, in a foreign country, and with a whole tour of gigs left to play. The best we could do was wait for help and deal with everything one step at a time.

A cop showed up quickly and calmed us all down. Apparently, accidents happen there all the time, like a regular Tuesday lunch special. He helped drive our things over to the outdoor stage and called us a tow truck. We even had a pleasant conversation about music. It turned out he loved jazz, so I gave him a few of my CDs as a gesture for, you know, coming to our rescue and all.

On the bright side, all this happened right in front of our first venue, so we could play at least *one* more gig. We were shaken and apprehensive about what was to come, but still managed to perform a couple of sets of music. I remember being on stage, still shaking from the accident, and seeing our smashed-up car above the tree line, being hauled away on the back of a truck. Yeah, I'd say that's pretty rock 'n' roll. Yet, it was surreal—serenading our car's exit with a musical standing ovation.

Once we'd made it through that gig, we wondered how we'd get to the next one. Thankfully, our friends John and Jill, who lived just up the road, offered to deliver us (and our things) to gig number two. They had two cars—a station wagon and a sports car—and it took both to get us where we needed to be. We crammed suitcases into trunks, balanced amps on seats, and poked instruments out of windows and sunroofs. Somewhere in there, we found room for ourselves.

Although we had calmed down somewhat, the future of the tour was still uncertain. But we got through gig number two all the same. Our buddy Scott Garrett generously offered us a place to stay that night and the use of *his* station wagon for the next few days, cementing him as either a great friend or a complete idiot.

The following few days were a logistical obstacle course as we jumped through all the necessary hoops to get another car and keep working. We showed up at garages, waited for tow trucks, sat in parking lots for hours, shouted at rental company employees, and, oh yeah, still had to play music.

Thankfully, our perseverance paid off. It took several days, but we eventually got another car and returned Scott's. We got ourselves back on track and finished the rest of the tour without incident. After a few months of paperwork, my credit card benefits even covered the damage, so I was off the hook.

The moral of the story? Totaling a car is stressful, surreal, and inconvenient, but it won't stop this trio. All's well that ends well, right? Just don't try this at home (or on tour).

The next story should've been a simple matter: a blown-out tire. But it turned out to be one of the most stressful nights of my entire life.

No Time to Spare

We were scheduled to play at 8pm at a club in Luton, England. Luton is a bit of a rough town, mostly known for its international airport and for recently having been voted "worst place to live in England." But the Bear Club? It's a gem. It has an amazing, dimly lit supper club vibe and a great listening audience. We were pumped to be back.

On the way to the gig, our friends Natalie and Anders invited us to stop by their house to meet their new baby. They lived about 30 minutes from the venue, and their place was on the way, so we figured, "Why not?"

And the Crowd Goes Mild

As we got off the motorway, we were driving through charming country roads—the kind that make you think you're in a BBC nature special and that Brits treat as their own personal race tracks. While we took our own time, a small Fiat came blazing around a corner and crossed briefly into our lane before righting itself and veering back into its own. Joe, our driver, swerved to avoid it but overcompensated, hitting the curb. *POP! Hisssss...* We heard it immediately. Our tire was flatter than a horn player on dollar-beer night, and the Fiat just sped away.

No problem. I can change a tire in no time. It was about 4pm, and we still had plenty of time to see our friends and get to our show. Joe pulled the car over to the shoulder, popped open the trunk, and dug down for the spare.

Lug wrench? Check.
Jack? Check.
Tire pressure gauge? Check.
Tire?...
Tire?...
Ummm, *tire?*
Seriously?

Everything needed to change a tire was there—except the damn *tire*. Just an empty space where it should have been. Now what?

I called the car rental company, explained our predicament, and they assured me a truck would arrive within two hours, along with a new tire. Cool. That still left time to change it, see a baby, and get to our gig.

So we waited, and waited, and waited some more…and still more. Finally, at 6pm, I called back and said, "Hey, you said a truck would be here in two hours. It's been two hours, and no truck." The woman answered with fake sympathy, "We're sorry about the inconvenience, Mr. Lenz. The truck is definitely on the way." I did the mental math, and getting to the gig on time wouldn't be a problem, but I wasn't so sure about seeing the baby.

Fast-forward to 6:45—no truck, and I was starting to get concerned. I called yet again. "Hello, you told me a truck was on the way. It's been almost three hours, and nothing." This time, a different fake-sympathetic voice said, "We're sorry for the inconvenience, Mr. Lenz, but the truck won't be able to make it tonight. You'll have to wait until tomorrow."

Say what?

You've got to be kidding me! All of that waiting… for nothing? Apparently, their idea of roadside assistance was sending "thoughts and prayers."

Perfect. We were stuck in the middle of nowhere with a busted tire, scheduled to play in an hour. We needed to figure something out—fast. Now I was in a full-blown panic.

Time for plan B. We found a secluded area along the road to leave our car for the night, and I sheepishly called our friends Natalie and Anders, whose baby we were supposed to meet. "Hey, ummm… we have a bit of a problem. Any chance you could drive us to our gig?" By this point, it was 7pm, the venue was a half hour away, and I was doubtful we'd make it in time.

About 20 minutes later, Anders showed up. We stuffed our guitars, suitcases, and dignity into the car and sped off. Thankfully, the club already had some of the gear we needed. Our car? Well, we'd have to figure that out another time.

Luton is a small city, but the venue is off the beaten path. We had trouble finding it, so we arrived *right* at 8:00—showtime. Dragging suitcases and gear into a club—at a full sprint, no less—makes for an embarrassing entrance. Soaked in sweat and still in our T-shirts and jeans, we found a large audience politely waiting for us. Never before had we set up so quickly, and we immediately began to play our set as if nothing had happened. All things considered— only 10 minutes late.

It was a small win, but this war was far from over. There was still a lot to figure out, and my mind was racing, thinking about all the details: how to get a new tire, how to get to our hotel, how to get back to our car, and every other difficulty that lay ahead. But it was time to perform and make music, so I put it all aside for the moment. Well, at least I tried.

To make things even more exciting, we had a hotel room booked nearby—about a 15-minute walk from the club. Check-in was by 10pm; otherwise, we'd have been homeless that night. There was no chance of checking in *before* the gig—we had to get right to work. After the show was too late. Which left one option.

After a frazzled first set, it was time to break. But instead of using that intermission to take a breath, collect myself, and grab a drink, I *sprinted* to the hotel, checked in, got our keys, then raced back just in time for the second set. It was kind of like a musician's pentathlon—or, better yet, a stress-athlon. Sweatier and even more frazzled than before, I picked up my guitar and went right back to work.

Sometimes, when musicians can't seem to focus well or are unable to find new creative ground, they'll fall back on the things they know will work and have probably played a million times before. Your hands play the gig, but your mind's in another zip code. This gig was performed entirely on autopilot while my head was busy composing a Blues in F—as in, "F my life." There was no mental space for creativity or imagination, but I managed to get the job done well enough under the circumstances, and my autopilot was promoted to captain that night.

After the show, we had no way to get to our accommodations, so the club owner took pity on us and gave us a ride. The hotel was a dive; the rooms were tiny, dilapidated, and suffocating on that balmy July night, but I'd never been more grateful to have a bed and the chance to lie down and rest. I was physically and mentally shattered.

When I finally checked my phone to catch up on the texts and emails I'd been ignoring all day, I saw that the battery was low. I searched my suitcase for my charger and suddenly remembered I had left it in the car. My phone was about to die, and I had no way of charging it. Battery at 10%; anxiety at 100%.

That threw a new wrench into things. Fed up, I shut my phone down and attempted to get some desperately needed sleep. But I couldn't. My brain wouldn't turn off. It became a 24-hour help desk for "bad decisions made on tour," working overtime trying to troubleshoot the entire situation. I didn't sleep a wink that night.

When morning came, the three of us gathered together to make a plan. We needed to check out of the hotel, so we brought everything outside and left James to guard it like a loyal sentry. Meanwhile, Joe and I called an Uber to find our car and get it repaired. It was a good plan. Except that when I finally powered up my phone again, the battery was now down to 5%—enough to book an Uber, but it wouldn't last much longer. Still, we needed it to help us find the car, so it became a race against time.

When our Uber arrived, we gave the driver a general direction and set off to find our car. I followed along on my phone, but by the time we reached the area, the battery had dropped to 1%—as had my optimism. I prayed it wouldn't die, or we'd be lost entirely. We spent half an hour circling identical country roads looking for anything that might spark a clue. The English countryside is incredibly tranquil, though I'd never seen so much beauty while feeling so stupid.

Eventually, my phone went dark, the Uber bill was climbing, and I felt desperate for some lucky break. Finally, Joe leaned forward and pointed excitedly, "There! I remember that intersection—the one with the funny tree!" It wasn't much, but it was enough. We retraced our path from the previous day, and sure enough, there it was. On the side of the road, deflated and pitiful, sat our car—exactly as we had left it.

It felt good to find our ride, but that tire still needed fixing. I started the car to charge my phone and began calling local tire shops, hoping one might be open on a Saturday afternoon. I found one about 15 minutes away. Thankfully, they had the right tire, but they wouldn't deliver it.

While Joe wrestled the old wheel off, I sheepishly made another call. "Hi, Natalie and Anders. Yeah, it's me again. Ummm... Do you think you could give me another lift?"

It serves them right for being our friends.

This time, Natalie showed up to take me and the old wheel over to the shop while Joe stayed back with the car. I got the tire fixed, Joe put it back on, and we were back in business. We drove back to the hotel to pick up James and our stuff, and the ordeal was finally over. Back on tour, we'd solved yet another Rubik's Cube.

Looking back, it was absurd that all this misery had been caused by a single flat tire. Thank goodness for the kindness of our friends, otherwise we might not have survived. Later, I sent them a gift card as thanks; it hardly seemed enough.

Blowout in A Major Double Flat

During our 2018 tour, we decided to take it up a notch and cross another body of water. We branched out from playing only in the UK to playing in continental Europe as well. It took a bit of figuring out: different languages, different roadways, different electricity, different breakfast meats. But it all worked out nicely. We got a great reception and have returned every year since.

On that tour, I had booked our European dates at the end so that, when we finished, all we had to do was drive back to the UK, return our car and gear, and fly home. The schedule was tight, though, and everything needed to go according to plan, because immediately after arriving at home, we'd have to get right back on the road for a weekend of gigs in New York. At the time, this seemed ambitious but doable—if you ignore sleep, jet lag, and basic human biology.

For once, everything on the tour went perfectly—and I mean perfectly. The gigs went great, there were no broken guitars, no missed ferries, no bandmates in jail. I was almost starting to relax.

Our last gig of the tour was in Luxembourg, and we had the whole next day as a travel day to drive back to the Birmingham area. It was a day's journey that included a crossing of the English Channel via the Channel Tunnel train.

We hit the road early for a long drive, with Joe at the helm, as per usual. I said, "Hey, man, want me to take the wheel for a bit? You can have a break, and I wouldn't mind taking a turn on these nice European roads."

He was happy for the rest so we switched places. I'd been driving for about an hour, enjoying the quiet ride when I made a rookie mistake. It was just wrong. I looked over at Joe and said these ill-fated words:

"You know, this tour has gone so well. I can't believe we haven't had any disasters."

It was a stupid thing to say, and it was like I chanted an incantation to summon a demon.

Fate didn't waste any time. Within minutes, I noticed an old, beat-up truck in front of us with a load of porta-potties on it (classy). It was wobbling like it had had too much "potty." Before I could say the words "that doesn't look good," a big metal pipe fell off of it and onto the highway. I had no time to react and drove right over it. That pipe turned out to be the truck's drive shaft, and it blew out our two front tires. It happened so fast, I couldn't have avoided it if I'd tried.

Thankfully, I managed to nurse our car onto the shoulder of the highway. At a loss for what to do, I tried calling the rental car company, and they politely informed me that getting help in Belgium, with a UK car, on a Friday evening was... let's call it "unlikely."

A stern Belgian police officer arrived and asked us for our international driver's licenses. Clearly, we hadn't done enough research. We'd never even heard of such a thing, so no, none of us had one. I wondered if he'd believe me if I said I left it in my other pants? He was not pleased, but maybe because he felt sorry for us, we got off with a warning and a reprimand to get that license (it's *still* in my "other pants").

He also helped us out by calling a tow truck, which couldn't come fast enough. It was a Friday evening, and we didn't know if any garages would still be open. With such a tight schedule, the stakes were high, as was my blood pressure. If we didn't get it fixed quickly, we would've had to leave the car overnight, find a place to stay nearby, miss our train, miss our flight, and probably miss gigs at home. And, as I've said over and over already... we don't miss gigs!

So there I was, sitting shotgun in a Belgian tow truck, watching the clock tick like it was a bomb timer in an action movie. The garage closed at 6pm, and we pulled in *right* at 6pm. I leapt out of the truck and pleaded with the mechanic to stay and help us out. I gave him my whole sob story, and he must've taken pity on me because he stayed and changed both tires faster than a NASCAR pit crew.

Back on the road, we arrived at the train station hours late and prayed they'd let us on a train (apparently, pity is an international language). When the woman at check-in let us through, we showered her with exclamations of love and devotion—she seemed suitably flattered.

In the end, we got back to the UK, caught our flight home, and made it to New York after all (albeit as zombies). I was eventually reimbursed for the tires by the rental car company, and it was another happy ending.

But lesson learned: Never announce your success prematurely. It's like waving a steak at a hungry lion while saying, "It's okay, he looks friendly."

If you've been following along, you'll notice that most of our troubles are related to our "tour bus," i.e., our car. The combination of thousands of miles, a carload of gear, and lack of sleep is a recipe for disaster.

Besides the major misfortunes described in this chapter, there have been lots of minor ones too. You know, backing into walls, scraping panels, and busting lights. And, because car rental companies will find any excuse to gouge you, we've practically become auto body MacGyvers, replacing taillights and hiding scratches and scrapes with a bit of touch-up paint. We've gotten away with it, too.

Well, except once—there was the time we spent an hour crawling through bushes in front of a car parts store, all for naught. Let me tell you about that one.

Reflecting on our Mistakes

We were finishing up our usual summer tour with some dates in Europe, at a club in the heart of Luxembourg City. Unfortunately, the front of the venue was on a narrow road that screamed, "Good luck getting through here with your car intact." Naturally, we had to load in at the front and scramble to get all our gear inside before the next bus came hauling down the street.

With the clock ticking, we moved quickly. Back and forth, we grabbed amps, pedalboards, CDs, guitars, and drum-set pieces like a well-oiled conveyor belt. Everything was *nearly* inside when an annoyingly prompt bus pulled right up to us, nose-to-nose. This

And the Crowd Goes Mild

was not an "Excuse me. Do you mind moving your car, please?" kind of bus. It was a "Honk. Shout, Move your #%€ car!" kind of bus.

With the pressure on, I grabbed the last few things from the car, threw them on the curb, jumped behind the wheel, and gunned it in reverse.

Speeding backwards, I had *just* gotten out of the way when the car came to a sudden stop, accompanied by a *crack*! My heart sank. Despite the backup camera, I didn't see the pillar-like traffic bollard just below its view. Although I was now out of the way of the bus (you're welcome!), I'd just created a whole new set of problems.

I went out to survey the damage to the car, and as expected, there was a big crack in the rear skirt along with a busted reflector. A mistake like that can easily turn a marginally profitable tour into a loss. I felt completely disheartened, but there was no time to deal with it—we had a gig to play. I parked the car nearby and tried to put it out of my mind for the moment.

The next day, we drove back to the UK to play one gig before going to Birmingham Airport to fly to our first ever performance in Northern Ireland. It was a busy end to the tour, with a lot of logistics. During the long drive, I called every dealership and auto parts store I could, looking for a reflector for this particular Vauxhall model.

Yes, I know, a reflector isn't that expensive. But our logic was that if we could fix the smashed reflector, maybe they wouldn't notice the crack in the car's skirt (wishful thinking). Even if they did, it was one less thing they could charge us for.

With only a short time in the UK, we found a Vauxhall dealer near the airport. We drove there and spoke with the clerk.

Me: "Yes, we're trying to find this specific reflector. Do you have one?"
Clerk: "I'm sorry, we don't have it in stock, but I could order it for you."
Me: "We're flying out in two hours. When will it arrive?"
Clerk: "In four hours."
Me: "That won't work. We'll be back again tomorrow morning. Could we pick it up then?"
Clerk: "Tomorrow is Saturday, and we're closed on weekends. Could you come get it on Monday morning?"

Of course not. We had to fly home early Monday morning. There was no chance they'd be open yet. We thought it over, and I threw a Hail Mary.

Me: "Could we order the part *now*, and when it arrives later today, have it left outside somewhere for us to pick up *tomorrow*?"
Clerk: (looking as if I'd asked for a unicorn): "I don't know if we can do that. We've never done that before. Hang on." (He checks with his manager.) "Ok. It's no problem. We'll leave it under that bush right out front." (Points to said shrub.)
Me: "That's perfect. Thank you so much! We really appreciate it."

And the Crowd Goes Mild

It looked like we'd found a solution, and we skipped out of the store, spirits lifted. We drove to the airport, flew to our gig in Belfast, and had a fantastic time. The next morning, we returned to the UK and went straight to the shop to pick up the part before heading to our final show of the tour that evening. We'd have time to install it the following day.

As soon as we arrived, I darted to the bush the guy had pointed to, praying the part would be there. I pushed aside some branches... nothing. It was a thick shrub—maybe I just needed to look harder. I dropped to my knees and shoved my head inside... not there. Hmmm... Maybe it was in a nearby bush. Nahh. *Still* nothing.

Around the building? Nope.
Behind a planter? Negative.
Under the mat? Nada.
Nothing.
Nowhere.

There we were, on our hands and knees crawling through bushes for an hour, emerging empty-handed and filthy. In utter frustration, I grabbed a greasy pizza box from the car and scrawled with a Sharpie: "We came to pick up our car part. It wasn't here. Thanks for nothing." I slid it under the door.

Must've been quite the Monday morning welcome for *some* parts guy.

I called when I got home and it turned out the part didn't come in until Monday. Yes, the fix was expensive. The tour ended up being a loss. But hey, at least we got a story out of it.

At this point, you're probably feeling like you'd never want to travel with us, and you'd be completely justified. I wouldn't want to travel with us either.

But our trouble doesn't stay abroad—it follows us home too. Yes, there have been plenty on American soil as well.

No Sleep 'til Poughkeepsie

I had a nice little weekend run booked for my trio: Friday in Montreal, Canada; Saturday in Saranac Lake, New York; and Sunday at a winery near Poughkeepsie. A classic "fun-on-paper" road trip. But it was February, so we were basically signing up for a scenic tour of frostbite and regret. (What was I thinking?)

We got an early start on Friday, bound for Montreal. We'd played there once before and were looking forward to arriving a few hours early to stroll the cobblestone streets of this charming city before our gig. It's a six-hour drive due north from New Jersey, and we had a smooth journey up the New York State Thruway.

When we arrived at the Canadian border, there was a long line of cars—an hour-long wait, in fact. When we finally reached the customs window, the officer gave us that *look*. You know the "What's up with *these* guys?" look. He inspected our passports, peered into my small SUV, and said the dreaded words: "Pull over to the side, please." Ughh.

Being told to "pull over to the side, please," is *never* because customs wants to gift you a fruit basket as a special welcome into their country. Instead, we were greeted by another officer who wanted to know why we had enough musical equipment for a small festival.

This is the kind of moment when our "brilliant" plan to avoid getting a proper work visa kicks in. We explained that we were just visiting a friend and might play a few songs at his party. Totally casual. Nope, we're not a professional band. I guess we thought that "We're three grown men, driving around with a ton of gear to play some guy's party" was less suspicious than "We're a band on tour."

Shockingly, he didn't buy it. After asking for proof of this "party," which I couldn't seem to find, he let us know that we were not welcome in Canada with musical equipment. But he cheerfully suggested that we pay a local storage facility to hold it if we wanted to try to re-enter the country. What a great business plan—let's spend hundreds of dollars to stow our gear so we can make $50 at a gig. Sure thing.

So we drove all that way and waited in a terrible queue, only to be rejected by the friendliest country on the planet. We usually don't get that reaction from people until *after* they hear us play. We considered all our options, including giving up and skipping the gig altogether, but as you should know by now, we don't miss gigs! Our pride was now on the line.

By some miracle, we have a friend who lives only 20 minutes away. Their advice: "Just leave your gear on our porch. We're out of town this weekend." Well, the club already had a drum set and a couple of amps. *Hmmm...* Leave thousands of dollars of gear on someone's porch? Guess that's exactly what we'd have to do.

We raced to our friend's place, dropped off our stuff, then raced back to the border. This time, we drove to a *different* crossing, about 20 minutes away from the first. This one was smaller and primarily used by locals. There was no line, and the officer barely looked up at us before waving us through like we were at a McDonald's drive-through.

All in all, we lost several hours during this whole debacle—so much for checking out the city. But we still made it to the club on time, played our gig, and even got paid. Take that, bureaucracy!

The following day was a Saturday, and we started it off with that walk around the city we had missed the day before. We enjoyed a yummy poutine brunch and hit the road for an uneventful drive back to the USA. We were booked to play at a nice restaurant in Saranac Lake, nestled in the beautiful Adirondack Mountains of New York.

After we finished, we loaded out and hit the road just as a few flakes began to fall. "Eh. No big deal," we thought. (Right. And the Titanic just hit a "bit of ice.")

We needed to drive about two hours south to a hotel halfway to our next gig in Poughkeepsie. Driving out of Saranac Lake, the snow grew heavier with every mile. What started as "festive" snow turned into "biblical." By the time we merged onto the New York

State Thruway, it was downright treacherous—some of the worst driving conditions I'd ever experienced in my life—but there was no turning back. We were determined to make it to the hotel, no matter how long it took.

Truthfully, there were moments when I wasn't sure we'd make it. I could barely see five feet in front of us and white-knuckled the entire drive as we inched along, mile by mile. We considered pulling over and sleeping in the car, but hypothermia was not on the itinerary. What should have been a two-hour drive turned into a four-hour ordeal, and we arrived after midnight, completely exhausted.

We were surprised to find the hotel to be a massive YMCA. It looked like someone had merged a summer camp with a government complex, and there was nobody around. I mean, *nobody*. I'd booked it online and notified them that we'd be arriving after they closed. They were kind enough to leave us a key at the front desk.

I was relieved to be there and desperate to collapse into bed. I opened the envelope with a key for room 312 and headed up to the third floor. As I approached the door, I could practically hear the bed beckoning me. Eagerly, I slid the key into the lock, and... nothing. I jiggled it, pulled it out, pushed it back in, moved it side to side, but still nothing.

Huh.

Maybe it was just me. When Joe got to the room, I asked him to give it a try. He pulled every locksmith trick in the book short of kicking the door down. Still nothing. I didn't understand. We were at room 312. What was wrong with this place?

Adding to the bad vibes was an ominous feeling looming over us. The hotel was massive, yet there was no one else around. Under normal circumstances, it would be charming and quaint. On this desolate, snowy night, however, it felt like I was in "The Shining," and I prayed we didn't suffer the same fate.

While Joe waged war with the lock, I called the "emergency number"—straight to voicemail. We stood at the door for 45 freaking minutes, jiggling the key in every way possible. Finally, I was done, ready to call it a night. I actually wanted to call it a lot of things, but I'll keep this family-friendly.

I said to myself, "Ok, universe, you win again. I surrender." I was resigned to sleeping in the lobby, which was warm enough and spacious with comfy leather couches. On a whim, I looked back through the envelope the key was left in. Inside was a folded-up piece of paper I hadn't seen earlier. When I unfolded it, I saw a map of the entire complex with a highlighted circle around a *different* building along with the words "you'll be staying here." I felt so stupid. We were in the wrong place the whole time! I couldn't believe I'd missed that.

We walked over to the *correct* building—the correct 312—and, *voilà*, the door opened as doors are supposed to. I was ready to collapse, yet we needed to be up again just a few hours later to get right back on the road. But there was still one final kick in the nuts awaiting us. That night happened to be the start of daylight saving time, which meant that we had to turn the clocks ahead, losing one more precious hour of sleep. What are the chances? My 1am bedtime immediately became 2am.

After a long silence, Joe mumbled from his bed, "We should have stayed home this weekend." I couldn't argue with him.

Alright. How about one last tale? This one also happened in New York—and, of course, a snowstorm was involved. Snow in New York is not measured in inches; it's measured in emotional damage.

Fuelish Behavior

We had a weekend of gigs in New York, with Friday and Saturday nights in Lake Placid and then a private Sunday gig on Long Island. For anyone who doesn't know the geography, that's like playing a doubleheader in the Himalayas, followed by a Sunday brunch in Brooklyn.

They're also about five hours apart—not taking traffic, weather, or bad karma into account. So I came up with the brilliant plan that, rather than leaving at sunrise on Sunday, we'd drive part of the way after our Saturday night gig and stay somewhere in between. By now, I'm sure you've learned that all my attempts to "make things easier" tend to make the universe laugh and say, "Hold my beer."

As we played our Saturday night gig, we were next to a large window overlooking the picturesque main street of Lake Placid. We nervously watched the weather rapidly deteriorate as a blustery snowstorm rolled in (sound familiar?). Sensing the urgency, we struck our last chord at 10pm on the dot, hastily packed up our gear, loaded up the car, and dashed off.

As I began driving, I noticed our gas tank was alarmingly low. I headed directly to a gas station on the edge of town, only to find it closed. Really? This place is a winter hotspot, yet no snow bunnies needed their Subaru or Range Rovers filled up past 10:00?

Having struck out, we continued on, hoping to find something along the way, preferably sooner than later. Things were going from bad to "why did I get out of bed today?" as snow piled up quickly. Add to that the ice and fierce winds and it was starting to look like a scene that would frighten even the Donner party.

After leaving civilization, not much was around and I was worried. Joe started googling gas stations from the passenger seat, but cell service was so weak that it made me miss phone booths, and he was coming up with nothing.

To make things worse, the low fuel light began flashing, just to remind me what poor decisions look like in real time. Still, we're road warriors, and we were going to press on. I drove painfully slow. Even in the best conditions, the Adirondack Mountains are not a good place to test out the "boost threshold" of your sports car.

I spotted a gas station ahead. Thank heavens, it looked like we were going to be ok. But as I got closer, I noticed that it was closed also. "Geez. It's Saturday night," I thought. "Don't these people like to party at Exxon?"

A snowplow was driving towards us from the opposite direction, so I flagged it down and asked the driver, "Excuse me, do you know of any nearby gas stations that might be open?"

His reply was alarming: "There's one up ahead on the New York Thruway. It's about a half hour away."

"Ok. Thank you," I choked, feeling my stomach sink like a rock. A half hour away was too far; we'd never make it. It was decision time. We could either stick it out and try to reach the Thruway, although I was almost sure we'd end up stuck in the middle of nowhere, or we could find lodging at one of the many B&Bs we'd passed along the way. We opted for the latter. I desperately tried calling every single one of them, hoping someone would answer at this late hour. Nobody did. I guess if you're out past midnight in a blizzard, the people of Lake Placid figure you've already made peace with your maker.

There was only one option left, and it wasn't a good one; in fact, it was more of a last resort. We drove back to the station we'd passed earlier to wait it out. Even though the station was closed, some lights were still on, and a sign read "hours: 5am-11pm." I parked in front of a pump, got out, and tried it anyway. Hey, miracles can happen. Haven't you seen "The Wizard of Oz"? (Spoiler alert: Dorothy clicked her heels and went home. I clicked the gas pump and couldn't go anywhere, but hey, it was worth a shot.)

Defeated, I slumped back in my seat, and we all tried to muster a little sleep for the next few hours. It was freezing out, and we put on every piece of clothing from our suitcases to try to stay warm. I started the car and ran the heat every hour or so, just to keep our toes attached. And, the car was so full of equipment that we had to keep our seats upright and sleep like frozen mannequins.

So, there we were, a bunch of grown men sleeping upright in a parked car, at a gas station, halfway up a mountain, in a snowstorm. This was where my music career had brought me. Truly living the dream.

After a miserable few hours, the station came back to life at 5am sharp. The lights flickered on, and the pumps started up with a clatter and a hum. It was a glorious sound. I jumped out of the SUV, filled up the gas tank with what seemed like liquid gold, and immediately got back on the road, driving with heavy, bloodshot eyes. Still, we were moving, and I hauled it to the hotel I had booked for the previous night desperate to grab a few more hours of rest. We arrived at about 8am, only to check out again at 10am.

I didn't get any.

We've learned the hard way: it's not about avoiding disaster, it's about showing up anyway. By the time we reached our gig—a small birthday party—we were gross, tired, and dispirited. The audience never knew it, of course. Yup, folks, *there's no business like show business.*

9

With a Little Help from My Friends

Not surprisingly, musical nightmare stories aren't unique to me. Misery loves company, so I reached out to my musician friends, asking for their most absurd tales. The floodgates opened—apparently, everyone has *something* to get off their chest. Here are some of my favorites.

Kyle

It was an out-of-town trumpeter's outdoor, summertime, large-ensemble gig at Grant's tomb. During the last tune, he took a solo and started heading into the crowd, New Orleans style. Everyone was digging it. The band was vamping, vamping, vamping…

Turned out, the MF'er had bounced to his car and left with all the money for the band! I tried to find out who he was, but everyone was, like me, a second or third-string sub, so nobody knew this cat.

Jon

About 25 years ago, I was playing a production of *Jesus Christ Superstar*. The guitarist, Rick, was great, and we'd jammed a lot before the show. One day, we started playing some Brazilian music and discovered that we were both deeply into the genre. A few days later, he asked me if I was available on New Year's Eve; he had some Brazilian musician friends who were looking for a drummer.

The bass player had already booked me for another club gig playing a pretty typical American-style New Year's Eve party. It was a high-end gig that paid well, but I was tired of just "jobbing" all the time. I thought, *What if I finally follow my heart and play music I love?*

Despite the lower pay, I found someone to cover the high-paying gig. I contacted the Brazilians and brought a small rehearsal drum kit to their place in Queens. They were lovely people, a small band of vocals, accordion, and guitar. I'd play drums and percussion. We hit it off right away. They were playing Brazilian classics and said that's all we'd be performing on New Year's Eve, but we'd also do one set backing a separate singer.

When she showed up to go through her set of standard Bossa Nova tunes, things started to go a bit south. She was a mediocre singer at best, but I thought, *I've backed many mediocre singers; how bad can it be? I get to play music I love with good musicians, and hopefully it will lead to more gigs like this.*

So we went to the restaurant, which was lovely. The staff was extremely friendly, and they promised to feed us and let us drink as much as we wanted. They were happy to have us.

We got through the set with the bad Bossa singer, a pretty gal, who looked sexy and made sultry Bossa Nova sounds, so the crowd loved her. It was embarrassing, but fine.

We started our set, and I was having a lot of fun and was glad I'd taken the gig. Further into the set, members of the audience start yelling out song requests. The host approached us and asked, "Do you guys know any other types of music?" Somebody in the crowd overheard this and yelled, "Yeah, play some jazz."

The accordion player looked back at me, panicked, and said, "You mean like swing?" He looked absolutely terrified. I replied, "Yeah, do you know any jazz tunes?" He was completely frozen, so I said, "Let's play Blues, just pick a key."

The two musicians were still in panic mode. The crowd, who had stopped dancing and were staring at us, weren't being mean; they just wanted to hear something else. It was New Year's Eve, and they wanted to party and dance.

All of a sudden, a light bulb went off and the accordion started playing the opening measures of "In the Mood" by Glenn Miller. This was great, and I joined in on the hi-hat. The guitarist smiled and enthusiastically started playing along, except that the accordion was only playing the first two measures over and over and over again. That was all he knew.

The two of them were now in bliss mode, because upon hearing this, the audience cheered and resumed dancing. But he didn't deviate from the one-chord riff. I was calling out chord progressions, but they weren't responding. I completely blocked out the rest of the night. I must've just started drinking heavily. We were a few floors above the street, and there was a big glass window behind me. I considered jumping out of it and leaving my drums there.

I remember that we got paid, but I honestly don't remember anything else. When I went back to the show a few days later and told Rick, he fell out laughing. I have many Brazilian friends and have played many gigs with them since that fateful night.

Nigel (originally appeared in the UK Jazz News and reproduced with permission)

I was booked to play at a wedding out in Buckinghamshire about 20 years ago. I know it was 20 years ago because I had this ghastly silver Ford Sierra with shiny silver hubcaps. The sat nav took me up a country lane in a forest, and I turned into the car park when I saw some balloons, but the actual venue was about a quarter of a mile away at the bottom of a freshly harvested cornfield.

I couldn't walk all my gear that far, so I asked a guy if I could get closer. He said that some people had just driven across the field and parked down by the marquee, so I decided to go for it. I quickly realized that the muddy terrain wasn't suitable for regular cars, but I couldn't turn around because the hill was too steep. As I got within a couple of hundred yards of the marquee, I saw the other vehicles and realized they were all huge 4x4 affairs. I also learned, with alarm, that there seemed to be a mound of earth and a ditch surrounding the venue that I would have to cross. I began to feel this rising panic and had to make a decision—stop...or speed up and, er, jump it?

In the heat of the moment, I went with option two and stomped on the accelerator.

It was at that moment that I passed the edge of the forest on my left, revealing the sight of the entire wedding party of maybe 150 people in suits and dresses on a huge veranda. They all stopped with champagne in hand, and gaped incredulously at the silver chav wagon thundering across the field with the noise of the corn stalks whipping at the bodywork. It sounded like machine gun fire.

The mound was coming up. I was fully committed. No way back. I actually hit the mound with the belly of the car, causing a huge metallic booming sound. Time seemed to stand still as I jumped the ditch like something out of *The Dukes of Hazzard* and thumped down on the grass on the other side, sending guitars, amps, and limbs flying in all directions inside the car. I managed to keep control, though, and calmly pulled up between two Range Rovers. Nobody said a word. I had to get a tractor to drag me out later.

Heather

I am a piano player and keyboard player. While I've played at many weddings, one in particular stood out. What was scheduled to be a two-hour reception turned into nearly eight hours of some weird revival situation where people were speaking in tongues and kept asking me to stay and keep playing. In retrospect, I should have left.

At the end of the gig, the groom "lost his wallet" and didn't pay. But later that night, after I had left, he called, wanting me to meet him at 3am somewhere because they were leaving for their honeymoon the next day. We arranged a more decent morning-time meetup, and he actually paid, but the whole thing was so odd!

Joe

There was a gig in Pennsylvania, in Amish country somewhere. We were playing as a jazz quartet for someone's wedding, and it was outside on a beautiful property. It was a wide-open space, no trees around, and we played under a giant tent with no sides. I mean, the center mast had to have been, I don't know, fifty feet tall. It was huge.

And the Crowd Goes Mild

While we were playing the cocktail hour, the sky was beautiful; it was a perfect day. As we finished our first set, the sky grew darker, first turning gray and then brown. The wind started kicking up, and it began raining. It quickly turned into a downpour, raining so hard that it was actually coming down sideways into the tent.

Everybody was panicking. All our gear started to get wet, and I remember pulling our amps and drums towards the center to try to keep them dry. The tops of the tents were filling with so much water that they looked like they were going to collapse. People were pushing brooms to push the water over the sides, and it was just cascading down. There was mud everywhere. It was a mess.

The power went out, and the wind kicked up so hard that I was convinced that the tent was going to fall over. If it did, people would die, considering its size. It was absolute insanity, and I remember the bride running around in her white wedding dress—now completely brown from the knees down because of all the mud. We didn't know whether to go outside and possibly get wet or struck by lightning, or stay under the tent and risk having it collapse on us. Thankfully, the storm passed as quickly as it came, yet they couldn't get the power back on, so they let us go home early. Man, it was like being in "The Wizard of Oz."

Megan

The first time I played at a specific diner, a toddler walked up to me, took my tip money out of the jar, and started playing with it, throwing it around. At the same time, her older sister got up from the table and started dancing to my music while they *both* threw my money around.

Meanwhile, their dad was at the bar ordering a drink while their mom was sitting at the table looking like she was about to have a nervous breakdown. When I finished my song, I had to get into teacher mode and tell the girls that it was real money and I needed it back.

Later in the night, a crew of drunk guys came in. One of them came up and interrupted me in the middle of my song, asking me a ton of questions. He then sat down next to me and tried to take my guitar because he said he "plays too."

Throughout the night, he kept coming up to me, then said, "My girlfriend is getting seriously jealous that I'm hitting on you." I looked over at the bar, and sure enough, she was glaring at me. I told him that he'd better get back to the bar and leave me alone because I didn't want any trouble. I couldn't wait for that gig to end.

Larry

During my last contract as a showband guitarist for Carnival Cruise Line, they hired a drummer who sounded like he had bought sticks on the way to the ship that afternoon. He was awful, and I had two weeks left in my contract. He didn't get better, and also had an attitude about it. His wife was the cruise director, and he'd signed on for a six-month contract to be with her, even though he couldn't play at all.

He was a drummer with no time! Forget about faster or slower tempos, or playing a production show to a click track; he managed to turn the time around and pull the tempo into a ditch every time we played. That was the first time I was truly embarrassed as a performing musician, so I thought of the gig as an entertainer, connected with my inner David Lee Roth, got a wireless, and started running around, taking solos while lying on my back in front of the big band. Passengers were showing up and giving me Red Bulls to see "what Larry would do."

I tried to get fired and couldn't. That was my last ever contract as a cruise ship showman musician.

Tom

About a year after I graduated from college, I was playing around Boston with a band called Third Estate, which played "world beat" music—basically funk with reggae, calypso, and Latin influences. We were playing at a club a block away from my apartment; I could literally see it from my window. I think it was owned by some of the guys from Aerosmith, and I was excited to play there.

We went in the afternoon for a soundcheck, which went well. Afterwards, I walked back to my apartment to have a break, and about a minute after sitting down for dinner, I heard a bunch of fire truck sirens in the distance. They were getting closer and closer, and eventually turned down my street. I wondered what was going on. It would've been really crappy if it were something in my building, but there was no way the club could be on fire. I laughed off the thought.

I finished my dinner and headed back to the club. Sure enough, when I got there I saw smoke pouring out of the front door. Of course, the gig was cancelled. Thankfully, all of my gear was ok.

Mike

I was doing a gig with an eight-piece function that I used to run with a friend of mine. It had a rhythm section, three horns, and vocalists. We were performing at a corporate event, so we set up on the stage, did the sound check, and everything was fine.

We started the gig and were four or five numbers in when I saw a woman quickly approaching the side of the stage. I was watching her, thinking, "She's coming over here. She's coming over." While we were in the middle of a tune, she walked up the steps, and I thought, "What's she going to say to me?" She walked straight past me, across the stage, and down the other side of the steps. I thought it was quite weird, but after the gig, the guitarist asked, "Did you see that woman? I said, "Yeah, what was she doing?"

He said, "She walked across the stage and started unplugging all the plugs and all the power. She was just unplugging everything and then stormed off."

Somebody told us afterward that the back wall that we were playing against was a temporary door—the kind you can pull backward and forward. On the other side was a quiet award ceremony. They were in the middle of their ceremony when an eight-piece soul band started playing, and their entire event had to stop and move. I don't know what she unplugged, but we never lost power!

Gary

My band was set to play at a big Mexican restaurant near Stoney Point, New York. The place had several rooms, so it was almost like a private party with our fans. There is often a roving Mariachi band at Mexican restaurants, and just as we were set to go on, a Mariachi band made its way into our room and wouldn't leave.

So our singer started dancing near them, subtly encouraging them to leave. When that didn't work, she literally pushed them out while she danced.

Tom

This goes back about a dozen years or so. I was with my band, which is primarily a jazz fusion trio; occasionally, we have people sit in with us. We used to play at a place called the Chocolate Moose. It was a coffeehouse that was jazz and blues-friendly. A lot of students used to go there to hang out.

One time, halfway through our first set, a guy walked in, and I could tell he was agitated. I thought I recognized him, and put two and two together, realizing he worked there. I found out that he'd been fired the night before for being generally unfriendly and snarky toward customers.

When he initially arrived, things were calm, but it wasn't long before they started to escalate and foul language began to fly. People stopped what they were doing, directing their attention towards him and away from the music. At that point, the band had stopped playing. I was in the middle of a piano improvisation and introduction to the next piece, but it had become extremely uncomfortable because the guy was playing so loudly.

As a side note, I grew up in my dad's movie theater in the Wilkes-Barre, Pennsylvania area, so I'd heard so many cartoons, movie soundtracks, and incidental music that, over time, they inhabited me. I said, "The heck with it. Nobody's paying attention to what I'm doing; they're just focusing on this guy." So I started playing music that fit the situation. People began to understand what I was doing and started laughing. I was like, "OK, let me keep going with this." The police eventually arrived, and I added more dramatic music by incorporating string sounds and other elements. It was sort of like watching a movie unfold. When the cops brought him outside, I played the theme from "Dragnet," which got a huge laugh.

Geoff

I played with a NYC-area wedding band a few years back. The bandleader was famous for keeping the actual gig times secret. She'd get everyone to the gig several hours before they were supposed to start, even though no one knew when they were supposed to start or end. Even worse was the lack of information when we went out of town. For this specific gig, all we knew was that we were flying into Myrtle Beach to play a wedding. She booked us on Spirit, the awful budget airline, while she was already going to be down south, vacationing with her family.

She hired a sound guy who would drive an equipment truck down and told us to bring all our bags and suits to the truck. It was an inconvenience not only to do the drop-off but also to do the pickup after the trip. Spirit charges for everything, and the bottom line was that she didn't want to pay for any check-in or carry-on bags. I was not about to put my $8,000 1957 Selmer Paris alto saxophone on the truck, which meant I would have to pay a $55 carry-on fee. I had to fight her for it, but eventually I was reimbursed.

Nearly everyone in the band was above average in size, so we were terribly uncomfortable during the flight, packed in like sardines. While on the flight, one of the male singers announced, "Check your emails" because the band leader had sent an itinerary. We discovered that the gig wasn't in Myrtle Beach; it was actually about three hours away, outside of Charleston, South Carolina. The plan was that they would pick us up by van and drive us to a hotel. But when our flight arrived and we were picked up, we found out we were driving two hours to the hotel, which, according to Google, was not north but west of the gig. WTF?

By the time we got to the hotel, it was already around 11pm, and she told us we would have to meet in the lobby at 7am to drive two hours for a sound check. The wedding was in the evening, so it was unclear why we had to leave so early. We arrived around 9:30am at a plantation outside of Charleston where the wedding was to be held outdoors in a wide, clear-frame tent that, during the day, doubled as a greenhouse. It was already so hot, and there were hundreds of dead dragonflies and other bugs littering the stage. The sound guy had just arrived, so we had to wait for hours for everything to be set up. When it was finally time to do our soundcheck, it was way too hot.

We played a few bars of the first dance, but that was all we could tolerate. We were drenched in sweat with no place to shower, and there was nothing in the itinerary about where we would be staying after the gig. After the sauna of a soundcheck, we still had about five hours until the reception started. The leader announced to everybody that the client would not be feeding us, so we drove into Charleston to find somewhere to eat. Our choices: Burger King, Popeyes, or Chipotle. For me, Chipotle was the healthiest option, so that's what I went with.

After dinner, we spotted a CVS across the street and ran over to buy wipes to "freshen up" before changing into our tuxedos. Fortunately, the gig itself went off without a hitch other than the post-dinner, two-and-a-half-hour marathon set. The gig ended around midnight, at which point we had to load all our equipment back onto the truck before jamming our smelly selves back into the Econoline van to drive two and a half hours back to Myrtle Beach.

The drummer was the chauffeur, and I remember being worried that he would fall asleep at the wheel. He kept whacking the top of his head to stay awake.

We finally got to Myrtle Beach International Airport around 3am and pulled into a parking lot. I asked, "Now what?" and the leader replied, "Now we sleep." I replied, "What? I can't do this." I hopped out of the van and started walking towards the airport to see if there was an open door. The rest of the band followed me like I was the Pied Piper. To my surprise, there was an open door, so we hung out in the front lobby of the airport while waiting several hours for security to open. Finally, six hours after arriving at the airport, we were on our flight back to New York.

When I received payment for the gig, it turned out to be only $100 more than what I would've made with the same band had we stayed home and played in the tri-state area. Never again!

Jeiris

I was playing music at a nursing home, and an 85-year-old woman started trying to twerk on me while I was performing. She kept moving closer until I was pinned against the wall, and instead of coming to help, the nurse laughed. My wife now refers to her as my girlfriend.

Lelica

One of the worst gigs I ever played was a corporate event at a venue in Basking Ridge, New Jersey. The woman who hired us was so nasty that she sent someone else to tell the bandleader she didn't like the way I was singing and wanted me to stop immediately. I was about eight months pregnant and very hormonal. I thought I sounded pretty decent, all things considered. Everyone else seemed to be enjoying the music.

The bandleader was apologetic and asked me to sit outside the room for a little while, saying he would call me back during the last set. I sat in the bathroom and cried. People from the event kept coming into the bathroom, apologizing and telling me they thought I sounded great and that I shouldn't worry. I barely sang, and they felt terrible. I got paid, went home, and tried to forget about it.

The following year, that bandleader was contacted by the same company, which asked whether we could play again. He said, "Absolutely not. I rarely turn down clients, but you made my singer cry, and we've never had anyone treat our band that way before in our lives." It was definitely a bit of revenge not to have to play for that woman again!

Steve

We were doing a jam set, and it was me on bass, a piano player, a guitarist, and a drummer. The place was packed, and there wasn't much room between us and the bar; we were kind of squeezed in, but it was fun, and we were having a great time.

One guy got terribly drunk, and kept bumping into the guitar player who was right in front of us. There was only room for one or two people to nudge by. He was in the middle of everything, and he kept doing it. Then he got close to my bass, which was when I forgot all that "be on your best behavior" stuff. I shoved him from where I stood right into the bar.

I had my only great bass in my hand, and the place was packed. He was so drunk that it didn't matter. His wife was sitting right there and got totally pissed at me, so we started yelling back and forth. It felt like a David Lynch movie. It became a big melee, and finally people dragged him out of the bar. Then, as they were dragging his wife out, she broke loose and coldcocked me in the side of the head. I was wearing horn-rimmed glasses, and she hit me right on the side of them. They bumped into my nose, and it started bleeding. I was still holding my bass, trying to protect it, with nowhere to go.

They then unceremoniously dragged her out. She was a large woman, and nobody wanted to mess with her. Later, she started beating her husband outside, so the cops took them away. When asked if I wanted to press charges, I said, "Of course not. I just want a good gig."

Matt

I was in my early twenties and had just been hired to teach guitar lessons at a local university. I was hustling, applying for grants and residencies. I wanted to be busy, playing as much music and doing as much writing as possible, so I applied for the National Park Service residency. Many national parks have this type of residency; you go, write music for a month, and then give a public presentation or something similar. Some of them pay a small stipend, and some of them don't pay anything, but they put you up in a beautiful place for a month where you can practice and write music, which is very cool.

I was accepted to one at Buffalo National River, which is in the Ozark Mountains of Arkansas. I was psyched. It was deep in the Ozarks, forty minutes or so from the nearest town. It was September 2005, and I thought, "Alright, I'll road trip down there, hang out in this cabin for a month, write music, practice my ass off, and it'll be beautiful. Then I'll give a public presentation, like a solo guitar concert, and come home to start teaching."

I was going to every jam session and open mic I could, and playing gigs in every possible context you can imagine. I was getting together with friends during the day to play music and practice, and seeing concerts every night. I was essentially running myself into the ground. I was also drinking crazy amounts of coffee and not nearly enough water as well as eating like shit. I was tired and had skin rashes. I never smoked or drank, but I did all the other things.

It took me a day and a half to get from Philadelphia to Arkansas. I was 24, and my head had been in the grind of playing music and networking for so long that I hadn't left the city in ages. So taking that road trip created a beautiful memory of getting out there.

When you exit the tunnels on the other side of Pennsylvania, it opens up and becomes the heartland. Then I went south through Missouri before eventually arriving in Arkansas and reaching the place where I was staying, a converted 19th-century horse stable. It was in the middle of the mountains and a short walk from the Buffalo River. The first day, I unpacked, got my guitar out, and set up my little space. I unpacked all my CDs and the transcription projects I wanted to work on. I went for a walk, and when I came back, I noticed a weird-looking bug bite on my right leg. Slightly bigger than a regular bug bite, it was a bit weird, but I wrote it off.

I had dinner that night, practiced, and did whatever else I needed to do. I woke up early the next morning, uncommonly early for me, got out of bed, put both feet on the ground, and fell; my right leg couldn't support my weight. Overnight, the bite had become infected. I went into the other part of the little house, looked out the window, and saw a park ranger making his rounds. I hopped outside the building and waved him down.

"I'm an artist in residence here, and something is up with my leg," I said. "I don't know what's going on; it appears to be an infection. Do you know where I should go? Is there a doctor?" He directed me to a walk-in health clinic in Harrison, Arkansas. It was so remote, about forty minutes away from anything.

I drove with my left foot to Harrison, got to the health clinic, and it was a total backwater spot. I'll never forget it. The doctor came out wearing a tie-dyed "Jesus saves" shirt with a giant crucifix over the top. He grabbed my leg and said, "What do we have here?" It hurt quite badly. He said, "It looks like you got a spider bite," and gave me an antibiotic. If I'd chugged the entire bottle of antibiotics, maybe it would've helped me, but it was a fraction of the strength I should've received.

I went back to the cabin and proceeded to get sicker than I'd ever been in my life. The medicine wasn't doing anything, and the infection was raging. I was in bed, in and out of consciousness, for a few days while my body fought what I'd later learn was a staph infection that got out of hand.

About three days later, I thought, "This is not right. This is not where I should be right now." I got back in the car, drove back to the clinic, and was told that I needed to go to the hospital because the infection had gotten a lot worse. I needed to make sure it didn't get down to the bone. The hospital did an ultrasound on my leg and saw that while the infection was not in the bone, it was still really bad.

I was put on another antibiotic strong enough to change course, but it still wasn't enough. I went back to the cabin and within three or four days, I was able to walk again, although I still had a noticeable limp. I got back in the car and drove all the way back to New Jersey.

There were long-term effects as well. When I got home, I saw a specialist who helped me. I got another infection about a month later. Then two more. Every time, I was in the hospital for a week to ten days. Over the next year and a half, I spent about two months in the hospital off and on. I had to leave Philadelphia and move back to my parents' house for a while to recoup. I gave up eating red meat and pork, cut back on the amount of coffee I was drinking, and started living a much healthier lifestyle.

10

Taking Care of Business

Most people play music for fun. It's a hobby, a stress reliever, and a socially acceptable midlife crisis. If they play out at all, a few gigs a month is just fine. It's like golf, but with a lot more gear. Me? I'm different. I'm a lifer. I caught the music bug early, and it bit hard.

Whenever a young, starry-eyed musician asks me whether they should pursue this career professionally, my advice has always been: Don't do it only because you love it; do it because you *have* to. By that, I mean you should only make this your career if there's an inner compulsion to play music and nothing else—as though not doing it will make your eye twitch involuntarily. You can always keep it as a hobby, and you'll thank me later when you have a 401(k) and can afford dental insurance.

If you insist on making it your sole livelihood, loving it alone won't be enough to handle the rollercoaster and the constant hustle. Once you rely on music to pay your bills, your relationship with it changes dramatically.

Q. How is a musician different from a mutual fund?
A. A mutual fund will mature and make money.

And let's be real: many hopefuls have no clue what a working musical life actually looks like. I want to shed some light on the realities of the hustle, the traits needed for survival, and career avenues you may not have considered.

For clarity, I'm not talking about musicians who exist solely in original bands. They aren't chasing the kinds of steady gigs I'm referring to here. Don't get me wrong, that world has its *own* set of challenges: getting exposure, the proverbial "creative differences," and navigating complex interpersonal dynamics—like discovering that the singer is sleeping with the drummer's wife.

Real bands are a dying breed, and they're complicated enterprises to keep together. Financial instability is a given, and turning any kind of profit is rare. Even when money does appear, there's no guarantee of an actual payday, depending on what had to be signed away to get there. And if any money *does* appear, disagreements over how to split it are inevitable.

Like everything else: mo' money, mo' problems.

No—this is about musicians trying to pay the rent with their instruments. Success isn't just about talent; it's about mastering a set of practical skills that keep you working.

Survival Traits of the Rent-Paying Musician

For mercenaries like us, you'll need the same qualities required of any job: reliability, punctuality, congeniality, flexibility, and the proper equipment. Whether you're a bandleader trying to keep a band working or a freelancer waiting for the phone to ring, networking and self-promotion aren't optional; they're survival skills. Think less "rock star" and more "socially savvy entrepreneur with an instrument." It's like being any business owner, but this business is built almost entirely on social connections, ability, and reputation. Being professional yet easy to work with will take you a long way.

Making the first contacts is tough, but going to jam sessions or showing up to other people's gigs can help. And yes, a little luck never hurts.

Talent matters, of course—it's the currency that opens doors—but it doesn't guarantee anything. Some have more than others, and those with little of it tend to blame the "evil music business" for their frustrations while keeping an unrealistic dream alive. Others make up for their deficiencies by being entertaining or charismatic; a memorable gimmick can go a long way. Unfortunately, my only gimmick is trying to play the right notes.

I know plenty of musical geniuses who barely work; conversely, I know some so-so players who thrive because they understand how to network and entertain, or have cultivated a unique persona or "shtick" that keeps them in demand. Maybe they tell great stories between songs, or take an awesome saxophone solo while walking through the crowd. It can be anything distinctive that sets them apart. Talent and ability don't always correlate with success—sometimes it's as simple as having a trademark style. People listen with their eyes as much as their ears, and it always helps to look the part—no one's captivated by someone who looks like they're about to sell you life insurance after the set.

Equally important, never underestimate the importance of being a good "set breaker," which really means being a "good hang." When we take breaks, some musicians like to grab a smoke or a drink; others prefer to schmooze with the crowd; but most of the time, we'll simply talk amongst ourselves, catch up, and have a laugh. Smiles, jokes, and a little camaraderie—they matter almost as much as your chops. If you're easygoing and your bandmates enjoy hanging out with you, it will go a long way in a field built on personal connections.

That should be easy, right: "Just don't be a jerk!" But we all know that some people simply suck at being a good person. Among the worst are the "Debbie Downers" who continually complain about every aspect of the gig: the duration, the pay, the songs, the drummer. The list goes on. It's a drag on everyone; if

And the Crowd Goes Mild

they hate the gig that much, they shouldn't have taken it.

Then you have those who constantly remind everyone who they've played with and use that to "vibe" with other musicians. It's one thing to tell us about the huge tour you were just on; of course, we all want to hear about that. But when it's used as a weapon to demean others or feed their egos, that's when I find it distasteful. Sometimes, it's even used as an excuse to boss or bully others in the band.

Another hazard of the job is being pigeonholed into a single style or genre. I know musicians who only want to play one thing, but I love to mix it up. If it grooves, I'm there. Because I play a lot of jazz, many folks think that's all I do and won't consider me for other opportunities. I guess I've got musical commitment issues—I just can't stay faithful to one style. But bouncing around can also turn people off who want you to stay in one lane. Jazzers think I'm too rocking; rock players think I'm too jazzy. At this point, I've managed to disappoint everyone equally. I wouldn't trade it, though—life's too short to play the same twelve bars forever. Variety keeps it fun and keeps me working.

Be warned: You'll also need to build up a thick skin for all the times you'll hear "no" along the way. Rejection is the norm. Ironically, you'll face more of it when you're starting and are least equipped to handle it. But the more seasoned you get, the easier it will be to take it in stride. It never ends, and it's hard not to take it personally. But over the years, the ratio of "yes" to "no" will slide in your favor. You can't let it stop you. You have to be relentless, almost to the point of being a pest—living in the sweet spot between determined and restraining order.

It'll help significantly if you can learn (and sometimes memorize) songs quickly and accurately. I've often been asked to learn a sizable number of songs, sometimes at the last minute—whether for a new gig, an original artist, or covering someone who needs a last-minute substitute. Doing your homework and staying organized are essential traits, particularly when you get that text, "Hey, are you free tonight?"

Another underrated skill? The ability to play quietly. It's not sexy. I know, but it will pay off. This is especially true for drummers and horn players who don't have volume knobs on their instruments. It's common to be asked to keep it down. Sometimes you wonder why anyone wanted a band at all! Nevertheless, even though it's fun to crank it to "eleven," if you want to keep working, you're going to have to dial it back down to two.

The best drummers I know can bash through an arena rock gig one night, then play at a whisper for a jazz cocktail hour the next. That's the sign of a pro, and that sensitivity and flexibility will keep you employed. Some gigs demand high-energy, but many others just want background music, and the only crime you can commit is playing too loudly. So, sure, you can play Slayer, but make it a quiet Bossa Nova, smile while doing it, and you'll be just fine.

The Fine Print

There is also a musician's schedule to contend with. Your social life will take a hit. We typically work when others don't: nights, weekends, and holidays (New Year's Eve is a biggie!). If you prefer spending time with friends or your significant other on Saturday nights, this job isn't for you. I'm rarely home on weekends. And if you need the stability of routine, you might struggle with the chaotic schedule; it's not 9-to-5, Monday through Friday. It's driving somewhere different every day, at all hours, as well as negotiating the logistical challenges that come with being in the right place at the right time.

It needs to be mentioned—this way of life can be even more difficult for the *partner* of a musician, which is why many are single. It takes an extremely understanding person to deal with it all. It might look fun on the outside—going to gigs, watching recording sessions, and hearing music around the house. But the reality is, that novelty can wear off quickly, and the day-to-day living of such an unconventional lifestyle can put a real strain on a relationship. It's not just about nights and weekends away, but also relentless at-home practicing.

Thankfully, I found a saint of a person who has stuck with me through it all. From the beginning, my wife, Mary Beth, not only accepted my musical neurosis but has always supported and encouraged it. I'll admit, I wouldn't want to be married to me, and I consider myself blessed to have such a tolerant spouse. On a daily basis, she puts up with her grown husband wandering around the house with a guitar hanging from his neck.

Behind every working musician is someone pretending not to roll their eyes—constantly.

When single musician friends bring a new date to a gig, I can usually tell right away if there's any future to the relationship. If the date looks miserable and bored by the whole scene, it probably won't last long. On the other hand, they might enjoy it a bit *too* much, showing up to every gig with their musical partner in tow for the entire evening. Between us, I'm not sure which is worse.

If you're ok with all this—including the late nights and excessive driving—and you still decide to pursue this career, just know that it's always going to be a hustle, and many of your choices will come down to money. Most of the time, you'll have to choose finances over art. That might mean joining a wedding band, a really busy cover band, or a tribute band. As it turns out, the world thinks originality is overrated, but paying your rent isn't.

Even more likely, you'll experience a combination of all of the above. People ask me how many bands I'm in, and I never know how to answer. I'm in so many bands and play with so many different combinations of musicians that I've achieved full musical multiverse status. Even *still*, piecing together a living is a challenge.

Q. How is a musician different from a pizza?
A. A pizza can feed a family of four.

And What Else Do You Do?

When someone asks me what I do, I tell them and wait, curious to see their reaction. There's that brief pause while they decide: "Oh, cool," or "Oh... wow." It's like they're evaluating my credit score in real time. Then comes the inevitable follow-up: "Oh. And what else do you do?"

They're not wrong. Most musicians have a side hustle...or ten. Many try to keep those side hustles music-related by working in a music store (although those are slowly disappearing) or teaching private lessons. I never did this myself since I already had a teaching job, but I've been told that an entire book could be written on this topic alone. I'll let someone more qualified take care of that one.

I'd always had a day job. I worked as a math teacher at a high school in northern New Jersey for over 25 years. However, music has also always been a full-time job for me, so I've had two careers plus a family. Yeah, I've been a bit busy.

Teaching worked well with my schedule, aside from the painfully early mornings. Admittedly, it was challenging to get up for school after rolling in really late the night before—I was famous for grabbing naps in the faculty room. But I also finished by early afternoon and could make it to any gig with no problem. There were many days when I'd run to my car immediately after school and dash off to an early corporate engagement. And if I got offered something *during* school hours..."*Cough, cough*. I think I'm feeling sick."

I also had several breaks throughout the year that allowed me to tour (summers off, baby!). I'd fly in from somewhere late on a Sunday night only to turn around the next morning and jump right back into teaching trigonometric ratios. My bleary red eyes usually gave my schedule away to students and co-workers. "Rough night, Mr. Lenz?"

It was hectic, but I didn't mind the pace when I was younger, although I missed more of my kids' baseball games and school concerts than I would have liked.

I sometimes felt embarrassed telling my full-time musician friends about my other job, worried they wouldn't take me seriously. Musicians who have day jobs generally don't play as well and are perceived as being less committed than those who don't. I get that. I even have that prejudice. Strangely, however, having my teaching job made me work even *harder* to overcome that, and I never wanted it to be an excuse that held me back.

Plus, I genuinely enjoyed teaching, loved the people I worked with, and it helped support my family, for which I am grateful. It never stopped me from playing hundreds of gigs a year, and I rarely turned things down because of it.

But I'm happy to say that, after retiring from teaching in 2024, I was finally able to call myself a "full-time musician," a title I'm proud to have earned.

Dollars for Ditties

I even stumbled into a nice little side hustle of my *own*. As I mentioned earlier, I've released over a dozen recordings of my original jazz music and have been selling CDs at gigs for years. I recouped a good portion of my investment over time, but a real breakthrough happened when I learned about "music libraries"—companies that house a wide range of music, soundscapes, and sound effects for audio and video production. They are often used by music supervisors, the folks who seek out and secure music for films and television.

I mailed CDs to several of these collections, hoping they'd be considered for all types of productions, and over time, I largely forgot about it. Then, a few years later, royalty checks started showing up in my mailbox. At first, they were small—a couple of dollars here and there. But as time went on, they grew larger. I'm not talking retirement money, but enough to cover a few bills.

It turns out, my music had ended up in hundreds of TV programs, and I had no idea. I wouldn't have known except for the quarterly statements I began receiving, which listed the songs, programs, countries, and platforms on which they were broadcast. These shows included *Breaking Bad, Young Sheldon, Chicago Fire, MTV Cribs,* and *Here Comes Honey Boo Boo,* to name a few.

I used to joke that I would be downright insulted if my tunes ever ended up on the Weather Channel, because their music is so bland. But sure enough, a few of my ballads ended up in some of the *Local on the 8s* segments. Yeah, I was a little offended.

Apparently, I'm dull enough for people only interested in the barometric pressure.

But hurt feelings aside, it was all a win for me. I earned back the money that I had invested in my recordings by doing virtually nothing but walking to the mailbox. Again, I'm not talking about life-changing money, but over the years, it has added up nicely, and it came from music I had already made. Furthermore, having these TV placements all over the world looks especially great on my bio.

It's been interesting to see the variety of shows and contexts in which they've been placed. Most of the time, it's below dialogue and hardly noticeable. Other times, they're used as "elevator music" for scenes set in grocery stores, doctors' offices, and even a car wash, as was the case with my *Breaking Bad* placement. So, in addition to soundtracking the local weather, my tunes have apparently been deemed ideal waiting-room music. I've developed a bit of a complex.

I've never heard them for myself. I only find out months later through royalty statements or from friends who've heard them. I mentioned earlier how, growing up, I was a massive fan of the progressive rock trio Rush. They were my favorite band as a kid.

A friend of mine once emailed me a YouTube clip of their drummer, Neil Peart, being interviewed by rock journalist Eddie Trunk on a VH1 TV special. I watched it and thought it was great, so I emailed my friend back and said, "Hey, thank you for sending me that. It was a great interview." He emailed me right back and said, "No, not the interview. Did you hear the music in the background?" When I went back to watch it again, I realized one of my songs had been playing in the background during the interview. I was completely engrossed in the conversation; I hadn't even noticed. It was such a thrill to hear my music in a segment with a hero of mine.

Hilariously, the comments section was filled with people bitterly complaining about how annoying and distracting the music was during the interview. I agreed. It was intrusive and poorly placed. Still, cash is cash.

Back in 2020, I contacted one particular music library to see if they would accept my songs. They responded that they don't take original music—they create their own—but liked what I do and asked if I'd be interested in joining the team. Hell yeah!

That opened up another avenue for me as a composer. I brought in a great drummer/engineer friend, Kevin Soffera, as my production partner, and together we've churned out hundreds of tunes across a wide range of genres.

The process is simple: we're given a "reference" track with a specific vibe to match (but not copy). It could be a song we're already familiar with, or something already within their catalog. There will also be a short deadline to write, record, mix, and deliver a fully produced piece that's between 2:00 to 2:30 minutes. It's a tight window but I love the challenge.

With so little time to obsess over them, as I usually would with my jazz music, it's been a great lesson in making quick decisions and being creative on command. There's an understanding that we aren't being commissioned to create great art, just a functional bit of atmosphere. While I can be a little obsessive in trying to make each piece as interesting as possible, I've had to accept that not every song needs to be Stravinsky; more often than not, they just want something simple. Still, the work has served as paid practice in the craft of songwriting I've spent many years trying to master, and for that, I've been grateful.

We've made hundreds of these little ditties and have become a well-oiled machine at cranking them out. Most of them are blues- or rock-based, but we've produced all kinds, including reggae, indie, country, metal, and even one in a style called "hick hop," a cross between country and hip hop. You know, the kind of thing you could pop and lock to… in cowboy boots.

We became particularly adept at what they call "swag rock," a style of song crafted for shows aimed at a more male-oriented audience. For instance, we made a lot of music for shows like *Pawn Stars, Forged in Fire, Fox Sports, Street Outlaws*, and later seasons of *Wicked Tuna*, which aired on the National Geographic Channel and was a reality show about guys who fish for tuna. When they were finally able to land these massive fish on the boat, there was always a lot of cheering and high-fiving—cue my swag rock tune!
I love doing it, and for me, getting paid to write music is a dream come true. Truth be told, that avenue has recently dried up (for us anyway), and I can only speculate that AI has taken that job.

The Gig Economy, Literally

On the topic of money, like most professions, you have to start at the bottom, and early on, I took *anything* that paid. I now have the luxury of being more selective—and I no longer feel the hunger to play every night as I did at 25. Promoters will take advantage of a musician's eagerness, and the number of times people asked me to play just for "the exposure" is ridiculous. Ironically, those were always the worst. All I was "exposed" to were some empty barstools.

The modern version of this is being offered a gig solely for its *social media value*—say, a particularly scenic view of New York City—rather than being paid anything that might help cover your mortgage. "Hey, Wells Fargo, can I pay you in Instagram likes?" ("Sure, and we'll accept that in foreclosure").

Some people think that just because you love what you do, you don't need to get paid for it. I'll remind those people that I went to school for this, missed a lot of parties to get good at it, and don't give it away cheaply anymore.

Of course, people often wonder what a musician earns per gig. When asked, I'll turn it around to find out what they *think* I make, and they usually have no idea. Ok, I'll spill the beans. The amount of money I have personally made on a single gig has ranged from $0 to $2,700. It can vary dramatically based on where you live, what you play, and the level of your profile.

At the bottom end are restaurants and smaller clubs, which might pay you $100-$200 per person. Hopefully, they'll feed you too, which is a bonus.

Next up might be a bigger club, and if I were in a cover band, I would generally earn $150-$300 per night. Above that are private and corporate gigs. Again, this can vary *dramatically* depending on the type of music, distance to the event, and length of performance, but I've generally received $200-$500.

Lastly, a sideman in a wedding band can typically expect $300-$500. In all cases, however, the person who books the gig usually takes a bit more for securing it, managing logistics, leading the performance, and diplomatically handling all of the bridezilla's "suggestions."

You'd probably think, from what you've seen in movies, that musicians are commonly stiffed by clubs, especially since most venues don't work with contracts, just verbal agreements over email. Surprisingly, over the thousands of gigs I've logged, I can count on one hand the number of times it's happened. Once because a club had a terrible night and were on the verge of going out of business anyway (they ended up giving me half), once because an overseas club couldn't figure out how to wire me money before *also* going out of business (notice a theme?), and once because the owner was a jerk and I was new at this. Otherwise, I've been lucky. In short: I get paid…eventually…sometimes in cash, occasionally by bank transfer, but always by the music, which never reports *anything* to the IRS.

Here's a little anecdote about money. This was not the most money I've ever made on a gig, but for the time and effort involved, it was a nice payday. In my early days, I was just starting to play solo guitar gigs when a booking agent contacted me about a

And the Crowd Goes Mild

corporate event at the Mohegan Sun Casino in Uncasville, Connecticut. It was a super-easy gig: two hours of solo guitar for a cocktail reception. That's musician code for "play nicely in the corner while professionals network and pretend not to hear you."

The only catch: it was a three-hour drive each way. That's six hours of driving and a lot of gas to pay for. I thought of a number in my head that would make it worth it for me to do this one. I said to myself, "If he offers $400, I'll take it." When I expressed my concern about the distance, he said, "Ok. I was going to pay you $1,500, but I'll throw in another $250 for the drive and get you a room." I did my best to pretend I had to think about it, then coolly replied, "Ok, yeah, I can do that." This was a rare instance when the universe seemed to have made a clerical error in my favor.

Unfortunately, that kind of math doesn't come up very often—especially when jazz is involved. I've played plenty of it over the years. Outside big clubs and festivals, gigs usually don't pay very well—jazz has a niche audience and rarely draws crowds like cover or tribute bands. An organ player friend of mine likes to joke, "I play jazz because I have a fear of crowds," and another always quips, "I'm going to keep playing jazz until the money runs out." The truth of these statements makes me want to laugh and cry at the same time.

Playing creative music can be *personally* rewarding, but it's rarely *financially* so. This seems to highlight a general rule in music: the more artistically satisfying the gig, the less it pays. Play avant-garde jazz, and you might leave with spiritual enlightenment...and $7.

You *can* make money by playing jazz at fancy events—as long as you're willing to keep it nice and "polite" so people can socialize over top of you. But at least now you're getting *paid* for being ignored.

The oldest jazz joke in the world:
Q. How do you make a million dollars playing jazz?
A. Start with two million.

Of course, pay can increase significantly in the big leagues—touring as a sideman for a well-known artist comes with a weekly salary, per diem, and bonuses. I have many friends who have landed these coveted gigs, and the work is often feast or famine. They'll fare well when they're out on the road and working. Still, when they come home, they need to hustle up local gigs unless they're fortunate enough to be on retainer during the interim.

I've done a bit of this kind of touring, although not with anyone famous, and mostly enjoyed it. It can get tiring, though, with early flights, quick turnarounds, and too many hours in the air. Nothing prepares you for a 6am boarding call like a career built around playing past midnight.

Sustaining Notes

One lucrative avenue that *doesn't* require travel is playing in a Broadway pit orchestra, a union position with great benefits. Being just outside of New York, I've known several friends who have gone that route. The biggest downside is that a show can close at any time, leaving you out of work with little to no notice. One week you might have eight performances, and the next you're humming show tunes in your kitchen. Still, it's a solid "day job" if you can handle playing the same show, note-for-note, night after night.

I've also known plenty of people who've taken jobs on cruise ships. There are lots of perks: a steady paycheck, free travel, and all the buffet shrimp you can handle. Some friends have returned with many more stamps in their passports and an alarmingly close connection to rum. Apparently, "last call" often becomes the real encore—and the longest set of the night.

The money might not be great, and the quality of musicians might be suspect, but I could easily see the appeal of an all-expenses-paid trip around the world playing music. That is, until nightmares of doing the limbo while hearing steel drum versions of "Hot Hot Hot" make you wake up in cold sweats.

I haven't mentioned anything about being a classical musician, but that is a whole different world unto itself. Whenever I feel like I'm not practicing enough, I remind myself of what these folks do, and I feel like a slacker. The virtuosity required to secure a job with a professional symphony orchestra is immense, given the difficulty of the music and the intense competition. You're basically trying to beat out 100 other prodigies who've been sight-reading concertos since they were five.

But they typically offer great pay, health benefits, and—rare in music—a pension. They're so sought-after that you might literally have to wait for someone to die before a job opens up. So keep your eye on the obituaries as much as the "help wanted" listings.

The Price of Passion

But, all in all, the reality is that it's *terribly* difficult to make a living entirely from playing gigs unless you're willing to go on the road for a long time with a well-paid tour or piece together any combination of the options mentioned above. There's also the need for health insurance. You can see why most people end up taking a day job or having a "supportive" partner.

Q. What do you call a musician without a spouse?
A. Homeless.

While I never landed my dream of touring with Sting, having a day job gave me the stability to raise a family. I genuinely admire those who choose the more unconventional path, dedicating themselves entirely to music. It's a relentless hustle, often involving long travel, loneliness, and a life far from family-friendly. Finances are precarious—frequently feast or famine—demanding both frugality and resourcefulness. As a freelancer, you're constantly choosing which fork in the road to take, trusting that one gig will lead to another and that new collaborations will open unexpected doors. Survival depends on adapting to a constantly shifting landscape; those who diversify, evolve, and endure.

Yes, it can be an incredibly fulfilling life, worth every note, but it requires a level of courage, passion, and ambition few possess.

11

The Times, They Are A-Changin'

All jokes aside, professional musicians are in danger. The industry has been in decline for decades, and it's time to sound the alarm. This isn't a "get off my lawn" rant—I just want to paint a realistic picture of what it's like out there now, and how we got here.

De-composition

Technology has transformed every aspect of music—from production to promotion to consumption. Most of these changes have been to the detriment of the people creating it. Like the rest of the world, musicians have had to adapt to new realities or risk being left behind.

One of the first casualties of this shift has been musical composition. I've always been a student of songwriting, and I believe that it's just as important a skill as playing your instrument well. Great musicians are nothing without a compelling vehicle to showcase their talents—like a sports car with no wheels: impressive, but not going anywhere.

Much of this change can be traced directly to the recording process itself, which computers have revolutionized. Capturing and editing audio has become as simple as pushing a few buttons. There's immediate access to virtually any instrument, sound, effect, or loop. Anyone with basic software can create convincing tracks with just a few clicks and very little understanding of theory or harmony.

Even AI has become a competent composer. The upside? Anyone can make music now. The downside? Anyone can make music now.

This democratization certainly has its benefits, but increasingly, true experts are being pushed aside and buried beneath the sheer volume of amateur content flooding the market. As has happened in other areas of the arts, music has been devalued by its ubiquity.

Ironically, despite all the possibilities technology offers, our reliance on it has made songwriting lazier and songs more homogeneous. The complexities you hear in, say, a Beatles or Beach Boys song have all but disappeared. Tracks are now commonly built around a constant electronic "trap" beat, a few chords, and a simplistic melody (if there is one at all), with minimal deviation or development. As a result, much of today's music begins to sound the same; there are only so many harmonic possibilities within such a narrow framework.

I realize that there has always been a place for simple pop music and inane novelty songs. Simple doesn't make something bad, and I'm not begrudging that. I'm only pointing out an overall trend that is hostile to anything complex or adventurous.

It's also understandable why this has happened. Most radio stations are now corporately owned, with strict playlists and narrow parameters that define the style and length of the songs they play. I remember as a kid hearing a wider variety of music on the radio, which was more tolerant of longer songs and musical development. Some of the biggest staples of mainstream Rock FM stations in the '70s and '80s, such as "Hotel California," "Stairway to Heaven," "Bohemian Rhapsody," and "Born to Run" are epic songs filled with twists and turns that showcase bold musicality. Can you imagine any of those being introduced on the radio today? It wouldn't happen. Radio has lost much of its relevance, but streaming platforms aren't much of an alternative.

Streams Lost in an Ocean

No, streaming has only sped up this devaluation. In today's digital age, music is more accessible than ever before. At the touch of a button, you can easily find just about any song ever released by any band; we're talking about *millions* of pieces of music. While it's incredible to have access to it all, that ready access only diminishes its worth. I recently saw a statistic that Spotify now adds more songs every *day* than were released throughout all of 1989.

While it's essential for artists to harness the algorithms to rack up streams, it doesn't add up to a whole lot in the end. The amount of money songwriters receive from their Spotify streams is a pittance, between $0.003 and $0.005 per stream. This is way below what traditional radio paid at its peak.

Even worse, an increasing number of fake artists game the system—all while Spotify reported over two *billion* dollars in profit for 2025.

I've spoken to several jazz label owners who lament the difficulty of promoting new artists amid this glut, while major labels are simply reissuing old albums, outtakes, and live recordings that have been sitting in vaults for decades. As an artist, it's easy to feel that there's no point in making original music anymore when the world seems to have more than enough. It's nearly impossible to recoup the money you invest in creating and promoting it. And yet, it's essential to release new music to stay relevant and creative. I always come back to the conclusion that this is my art, and I'm going to keep making it, whether people listen or not—I *still* believe the cream rises to the top. Naive? Probably. Silent? Impossible.

Live Music on Life Support

Aside from the struggles on the recorded-music side, live gigs have taken just as hard a hit. I hear stories from older musicians about playing five nights a week in packed venues—a reality that seems all but gone today, unless you're working in a tourist hotspot. "Netflix and chill" has changed the economics. People don't go out as much as they used to, and the entire hospitality industry is feeling the pinch. As a result, many clubs are paying bands the same rates they did decades ago.

Smaller budgets mean smaller bands. It's common now for groups to play along with pre-recorded tracks to fill in the parts musicians used to play. But it's not the same.

With more competition to be heard and fewer opportunities to be seen, the question becomes: How does a new band or artist cut through the noise to get noticed now?

Anti-Social Media

It used to be that aspiring musicians would cut their teeth by performing relentlessly and practicing in front of a live audience. Record labels sent scouts into clubs searching for the next big thing. That process has now been replaced by Instagram, YouTube, and TikTok. You can go from your bedroom to stardom without ever leaving your house. But if all you want to do is make music, that might not be enough. You're going to have to reckon with also being a "content creator," posting shareable photos and videos that aren't always just about music.

That said, it's pretty amazing to think that you have the potential to reach anyone, anywhere in the world, without having some big PR apparatus behind you. Some truly great artists have undoubtedly achieved success this way.

However, it's also created a breed of musicians only capable of producing a one-minute clip of sheer virtuosity—bound to garner plenty of likes but lacking in musical depth. It's treating music like an athletic performance rather than a medium for creating art that communicates something meaningful. These musical gymnastics have become so commonplace that they're now, dare I say, *boring*.

I've seen 7-year-olds with better technique and who can play faster than I can as a 50-something-year-old professional. But today's ecosystem is engineering a musician who doesn't know how to interact with others and be creative in the moment, because they always play by themselves.

Don't get me wrong, the technical wizardry these influencers can perform is awe-inspiring if they're actually real (some have been proven to be fake). I've learned lots of great guitar tricks from some of them, but I don't think they're necessarily contributing to the betterment of the art form. One could argue that there is always a place for this kind of content, but, sadly, this is what music consumption has been reduced to in many ways.

Just as social media has transformed the way new talent is discovered, it has also changed the way working musicians are expected to be seen and stay relevant. I never imagined that a large part of my job as a musician would involve spending countless hours making digital flyers, posting gig pictures, editing videos, and responding to social media comments—time that could be spent practicing my instrument or composing new music. Some venues now even require a minimum number of social media posts to promote an upcoming show. Once again, this is the new reality of self-promotion in the digital age.

Venues often care about the number of likes you get more than your chops. Booking agents might be more interested in how many followers you have than in your actual talent. Record labels tend to focus on how many streams you've gotten rather than the quality of your songs. I've seen interviews with music executives who've flat-out admitted they're looking for creators who've already built a large online following, because they lack the imagination or resources to develop new artists.

It often comes down to cold, hard numbers, and those numbers are the metrics upon which you're now judged as an artist.

Lost in the Mix

I should also address the plight of commercial recording studios, an industry that's been decimated over the past few decades. Home studios have been a godsend for many musicians and composers who might not otherwise have had the means to make quality recordings, but the consequence is that it has put many studios and the professionals who work in them out of business. Not only audio engineers and producers but also the studio musicians who play on jingles, demos, and even full productions. Why hire an expensive orchestra when you can use samples? Why hire a real bass player when the EZ Bass plug-in does the job instantly?

To be clear, I'm not bemoaning this technology—it's fantastic, and I've used it myself. I'm simply pointing out the reality facing aspiring professionals: work opportunities are steadily declining.

Geez, maybe I *am* a grumpy old man after all.

Auto-Tuned Ambitions

Despite this bleak outlook, music and music engineering schools remain busy. Although there's far less work available, music programs are full of young hopefuls who have been sold on the dream of making music for a living. I cannot fathom taking on tens of thousands of dollars in debt for a music performance degree in this environment—it's not a credential that secures employment in the same way other degrees can; the music business doesn't operate that way.

I understand—no college degree guarantees a career, but this line of work is built especially on personal relationships and reputation. In all my years, no bandleader, producer, or agent has *ever* asked me where I went to school or requested my transcripts. They only cared whether I could play, whether I was professional, and whether I could be counted on.

Q. What do you call a musician with a college degree?
A. Night manager at McDonald's.

If formal education is guilty of selling the dream, television is its most dedicated accomplice. Shows like "The Voice" and "American Idol" only contribute to the fallacy that the act of singing, in and of itself, makes someone an "artist." What these shows really demonstrate is that an entire industry exists to take anyone with a shred of raw talent and a touch of charisma and build a full brand around them. Meanwhile, this person may have never played a real gig, has no idea how to connect with an audience, and possesses little, if any, artistic vision.

However, it doesn't particularly matter. A team of producers, songwriters, stylists, and publicists is waiting to provide the perfect image and thoroughly market-researched songs for a specifically designated demographic. They'll package it nicely for mass consumption, then ensure we all hear this drivel ad nauseam.

That may sound cynical, but I remain an eternal optimist. No matter how glitzy or manufactured the music world becomes, I'm certain there will always be an audience that recognizes authenticity and responds to the real thing.

Signal vs. Noise

Yes, I may sound like a grumpy old man mourning the "good old days," but this is my perspective, shaped by decades of making music. It was all different when I was younger. Playing the guitar meant so much more. Music meant so much more. We would spend hours listening to an album, focused on every note. Today, music is often just background noise lost among hundreds of TV channels, lifelike video games, streaming, YouTube, podcasts, and social media—all competing for our attention. Somewhere along the way, music stopped being the destination and became mere scenery.

I'm not railing against these from a standpoint of bitterness (Ok, maybe a little), because people will find other ways to occupy themselves and find fulfillment. There's absolutely nothing wrong with that. I speak as someone who loves this art form and hates to see it fade into obsolescence.

I'm convinced that nothing in this world can move people like music. I've experienced it many times as a listener and witnessed it countless times as a performer. And that's why, despite all the challenges, I'll never stop making it. In the end, no algorithm, play count, or manufactured fame can ever replace a note played with real heart and intention—that's eternal.

12

Don't Stop Believin'

Whether I chose this path or it chose me, it's a pursuit that has shaped the way I listen to the world. It's hearing music in the everyday—the rhythmic sloshing of windshield wipers, the whistle of a passing train, or the clashing melodies of chirping birds. It's listening to life and broadcasting back to the world the inner feelings that can't be put into words.

This profession is full of contradictions—the thrill of creating on stage, the joy of traveling to new places, and the magic of a band in sync, all while enduring long drives, rough audiences, broken gear, and endless practice. But it looks different from the stage than it does from the crowd.

You've probably watched a musical performer and felt some admiration, imagining the happiness that must come from showing off your talents to an adoring crowd. It can look glamorous and exciting, yet it's only one step of a long, unseen journey required to get there—one that I've detailed throughout this book. From the outside, your perception of what it must feel like is probably different from what it *actually* feels like on the inside.

For me, there's less basking in the glow of adoration and more quiet worries: "Will anyone show up? Will I play well? Is the sound right? Are people liking it? And is that particularly chatty fan going to corner me later to talk about their love of breeding horses?"

Of course, it's exciting to walk out on stage. There's a high from a great show and a warm reception. It's blissful to get lost in the music, and it feels terrific to be validated by an appreciative audience. Those moments make it all worth it. But you quickly come back to earth when it's time to pack up your gear and make a quiet, late-night drive home with the evening still ringing in your ears, only to enter a silent house with everyone already asleep.

One thing has always kept me going: the people—the friends and fellow musicians who share this life with me. For many of us, this work is also our social life and community. Most of my closest friends are musicians, and we'd rather play a gig together than drink at a bar or spend an afternoon on the golf course—apparently that's what people with free time do.

And the Crowd Goes Mild

I always hoped these people I admire would let me into their club. The best feeling is knowing they think I'm good enough to be onstage with them—even when I'm not sure I believe it myself. Playing together is part work, part fellowship, and all part of enjoying the company of kindred spirits who've also been called to this crazy pursuit. It keeps us young at heart, and most of my peers are still just big kids in the best possible way. I enjoy our set breaks almost as much as the sets themselves—to talk, catch up, and share a laugh.

Whenever I didn't have a gig on a Friday or Saturday night, I always felt a bit lost. I didn't know what "normal" people did on weekends, because I was always out working. When I was busy with gigs (and school), I'd complain about needing time off. But when my calendar started to look thin, I'd panic—gripped by an irrational fear that the phone would stop ringing. Human nature, I suppose.

I realize much of this book might sound bitter at times. It's easy to see why many musicians become disenchanted. Not me. It's funny to laugh at some of the absurdity, but I would do it all over again if I had to—because in the end, I simply love making music. It never mattered where it was, who it was with, or what we were playing, as long as it was good tunes, good vibes, and good people. Even on the roughest gigs, I remind myself that I could be doing far worse things. There are times when it does feel like real labor, but what profession *doesn't* have its challenging days? As my dad always said, "That's why it's called 'work.'"

The man was practical—pep talks weren't really his thing.

But I keep proper perspective: all I have to do is make some music and not dig a ditch or work in a sweatshop. And for all the rough gigs, I've had many more great ones—some even transcendent.

Q. How do you get a musician to complain?
A. Give them a gig.

I'm passionate about what I do. Some people feel the same about baseball; others about wine or travel. Passion can attach itself to nearly anything, and I've come to see it's both a blessing and a curse. It's a gift to have something that gives you purpose. I think the happiest people are those who have something to look forward to each day. On the other hand, it can be oppressive, particularly if your aspirations go unrealized, your thirst goes unquenched, or your devotion turns into an unhealthy obsession.

For me, that drive has been relentless, and I admit that honing my craft has been selfish work—the hours of practice, travel, and managing the business are staggering. I've always pushed myself musically and professionally, carving out a career in a fiercely competitive field. But the other side of this obsession is that it can breed selfishness and self-centeredness. While some of it is necessary for the job, a lot of it is toxic and unhealthy.

Ambition can take you to extraordinary heights, but I've also seen it consume people to the detriment of themselves and those around them. It can lead to narcissism, distasteful eccentricities, and repellent behavior. And sometimes, that might be what's needed to push their personalities to the edge to create the music they do, or achieve the success they seek. Or, they could just be an asshole—I've worked with more than a few. Either way, it doesn't make it any more tolerable. Looking back, there were definitely times when I didn't have the formula right myself.

When I was young, I naively believed that a life in music would bring me freedom and a carefree existence—the fantasy every artist is sold. I found the opposite to be true. It requires a discipline that can feel like bondage—constant, relentless practice. In my early years, I rarely had time for "normal" pleasures, such as casual socializing, hobbies, and idle weekends. I even struggled to take vacations without feeling guilty.

Over time, I've come to see that every life is defined as much by what it excludes as by what it contains. Those choices give shape to who we become. I'm not a "normal" person and never needed a "normal" life, but I have since found a healthier balance and broader perspective. Fulfillment, I've learned, isn't about having everything—it's about making peace with what you choose to hold onto, and living comfortably inside those choices.

I like to joke that chasing musical excellence is basically an exercise in feeling bad about yourself, and early on, it certainly was for me. I'd often walk away from performances disappointed, or beat myself up for not being further along in my career. I became neurotic and anxious, constantly worrying that I wasn't working hard enough or successful enough. I measured myself against virtuosos and often thought, "If I could just play like that, *then* I'd be happy." Imposter syndrome was a constant companion.

Now, I no longer harbor those illusions about being the "best." There's simply too much talent in the world, and greatness is subjective. What I've gained instead is consistency and acceptance. Even my worst nights now often surpass my best from years ago. Ironically, whenever I think I've played badly, someone almost always tells me how great I sounded. It doesn't make me feel better, but it's a good reminder that I'm my own harshest critic. Not every performance can be perfect, and that's okay—it's never for lack of trying. I still have my "I suck" moments, but I'm much kinder to myself now. And yet, it's the struggles, more than the successes, that have taught me the most.

While I'm always striving to become a better musician, I've learned to appreciate the climb even if I never reach the summit. To borrow a cliché, it has become more about the journey than the destination. The struggle keeps me learning, growing, and working toward something unique and authentic—it's no longer about being "the best." And I believe having a mission is what makes you feel alive.

This pursuit of mastery has taught me far more than just how to play an instrument. Along the way, it's given me skills that have made me a better human being—discipline, a strong work ethic, self-reflection, patience, cooperation, humility, determination, and self-acceptance.

I take pride in the progress I have made and how accomplished I've become. On rare occasions, I even feel like I've mastered this art and can play anything—but that feeling is fleeting and can easily be erased by the next gig. As they say, "You're only as good as your last performance."

I used to think success was something you arrived at.

Although I never landed "the big gig," I have friends who have, and I've seen firsthand that performing in front of large audiences or having perceived success doesn't automatically bring happiness and fulfillment. I've proudly watched buddies of mine, from the sides of stages, play arenas and stadiums with superstars. It's still the same job—just bigger, louder, and often with the same headaches. The truth is, music is meaningful at any level, from small cafés to big stadiums.

When I catch myself lamenting that my career didn't exactly set the world on fire, I remind myself that there is no singular moment of "making it." It's a collection of small, barely noticeable wins over many years that form a body of work and lead to the greatest achievement: simply being able to participate in this art and get paid to do it. For me, it's never been about being rich or famous; I wasn't interested in either. I simply wanted to be "successful," and over time, my definition of success has evolved dramatically. These days, steady work is an accomplishment easily overlooked, and I'm grateful to be getting paid for something I'd be doing for free in my basement anyway.

That realization has helped me see that I am lucky to bring something into the world that makes people happy (usually, anyway) while also providing an outlet for personal expression. At my core, I'm a huge music fan, so participating in it feels like a dream fulfilled. I'm still fascinated by sound, the mechanics of harmony, and the way certain combinations of frequencies (notes) can stir memories, feelings, and emotions within us.

I'm continually astonished by the new and inventive ways people can take the twelve notes of Western harmony and create something innovative from them—even after centuries of existence. (And yet, with all those combinations, the most requested one still sounds like "Sweet Caroline." Go figure.)

It ultimately comes down to expectations. Believing you deserve recognition or fame is a dangerous mindset, because the universe rarely delivers what we think we're owed. In popular music, success isn't always tied to merit. That's just reality.

I write columns for the website *All About Jazz*, and in one piece I wrote:

I find that the business can make people jaded and cynical. I've seen musicians become embittered about the gigs or the accolades they didn't get. This is so easy to happen as we often compare ourselves to others (usually more successful)... I've come to accept that we can't all reach the level of fame we imagine. For me, it always comes back to the core reason I started doing this in the first place: the joy of playing music. That's what makes me happiest and pushes the grudges aside.

And the Crowd Goes Mild

Musicians have a gift. When creating is at its best, it can make you feel like you've tapped into something cosmic, and is one of the most direct pathways to experiencing the divine. Musicians are part storytellers, part teachers, part preachers, and part shamans. To master this art is to connect with a wide range of feelings and communicate them to others, allowing them to experience them as well: excitement, sadness, joy, lust, freedom, melancholy, and anger, to name but a few. Imagine having the ability to stir a profound emotion in someone or evoke a forgotten memory. It's magical.

Then again, it can all come crashing down in an instant when you're asked to turn your volume down, play something people can dance to, or play "Happy Birthday" for the brat in the corner. Such is the music business, from hero to zero, just like that.

While the topic of this book is very specific—the occupation of making music—the themes are universal. True mastery requires consistent effort, sacrifice, and self-reflection. Dreams and ambition give life purpose and meaning, but they need to be tempered with acceptance and appreciation. Happiness doesn't come from fame or external validation, but from engaging deeply with your craft, connecting with others, and finding fulfillment in small victories. And above all—trust me—you don't *ever* want to travel with my band.

To my musical brethren: keep chasing your muse, embracing the grind, and savoring every triumph, big or small. To the "civilians" reading this, notice the devotion behind the music—the long hours, missed weekends, and rough crowds. Music is more than entertainment, and even a *little* acknowledgment means more than you know.

Someday we might cross paths—you might catch me playing "Livin' on a Prayer" at your cousin's wedding. If you do, *please*, I'm begging you: don't call out for "more cowbell."

About the Author

B.D. Lenz is a guitarist, composer, and producer based in northern New Jersey. *The New York Times* has noted that "part of the reason for his accessibility is that he not only fuses jazz and rock, but he complements it with the warm chords of funk, soul, and rhythm and blues." He has released more than a dozen albums as a leader featuring some of jazz's biggest names, has played in nearly every kind of band imaginable, and has produced recordings for both emerging and established musicians across many genres.

A seasoned performer with an international following, Lenz's music has appeared in hundreds of television and film placements worldwide, including *Breaking Bad*, *Young Sheldon*, *Catfish*, and *Chicago Fire*. He tours extensively throughout the United States, Europe, and the UK as a solo artist, sideman, and with his long-running trio. When not on the road, he can usually be found composing for Gramoscope Music or writing about the music business as a columnist for *AllAboutJazz.com*.

www.ingramcontent.com/pod-product-compliance
Lightning Source LLC
LaVergne TN
LVHW010320070526
838199LV00065B/5613